THE FINAL DESCENT

THE UNTOLD STORY OF THE FIRST RIDER
TO DIE IN THE TOUR DE FRANCE

MICHAEL THOMPSON

ISBN: 9798397034548

CONTENTS

For Paco and Alvaro

"The living owe it to those who can no longer speak to tell their story for them."

CZESLAW MILOSZ, THE ISSA VALLEY

Francisco Cepeda Nistal

THE FINAL DESCENT

Tour de France, Thursday 11th July 1935, Stage 7, Aix-Les-Bains to Grenoble

From Col du Lautaret to Rioupéroux

Paco knew how to suffer. Pride and dogged determination enabled him to endure more pain than most of his rivals. He had survived the hellish descent from the Galibier, with its terrifying twists and turns, but he still had the agonising climb to the Col du Lautaret, before the final descent towards the finish line in Grenoble. Several riders were strung out ahead of him, toiling against the incline, but Paco slowly worked his way back to them. By the time the riders crested the col, at two thousand and fifty-eight metres, the group had swelled to nine. There were some well-known faces and Paco was relieved to make contact with such a strong pack of riders. There was safety in numbers, especially in the final hours of a long and strength-sapping stage. This small peloton snaked its way down the dark and narrow Romanche Valley. After hours of climbing, gravity now became their friend as they sped through Le Grave, beneath the towering ice glaciers of the Meije. The gravel rushed beneath their tyres, as they descended at frightening speeds.

As the riders approached the small, untidy village of Rioupéroux, Paco was at the head. It was an illustrious group that he led in single file and at high speed. The remnants of the French team, which had nursed their captain, Antonin Magne, as far as the lower slopes of the Télégraphe, had come together; André Leducq, the winner of the Tour in 1930 and 1932, Charles Pélissier, already a winner of stage two, and René Le Grevès. Paco's fellow Spaniard, Antonio Prior was also present, as well as two Italians, Remo Bertoni and Pietro Rimoldi and two French touristes-routiers, Georges Lachat and Théodore Ladron. They were all riding to limit their time losses. To the right, and in the valley below, the riders caught their first glimpse of the cluttered roofs of the numerous paper mills, steel works and hydroelectric plants, hemmed in by the colossal but solemn mountain faces on either side. The Romanche was a white, frothing torrent of water, forcing its way between the black and grey rocks and the huge boulders which, over time, had broken away from the steep mountain sides, to find their resting place in the ravine below.

Paco had signalled to his compatriot, Prior, that, with just thirty-five kilometres to the finish, he intended to attack. He hoped he might close the gap on the leading riders, who were some minutes ahead, and improve his position in the overall classification. Recovered from his exertions on the Galibier, during the rapid descent from the Col du Lautaret, he felt renewed strength in his legs. This had been an immensely difficult and stressful stage, but with less than an hour of riding left to the finish, and the road gradually descending all the way to Vizelle, Paco was confident he was capable of a strong finish.

He knew this was likely to be his final Tour, and he had not given up hope of making it a memorable one.

Paco's legs were spinning as the small group flew through Rioupéroux towards the bridge at the southern limits of the village. There was a scattering of spectators on the roadside. They were mainly locals; some working men from the factories and some children, waving, clapping and cheering. Paco's eyes were fixed on the road ahead which he could see was about to arc its way to the right. He was hugging the right-hand side of the road so there was no more than a metre between him and the spectators. At over fifty kilometres per hour, they were mostly a blur to Paco. Most of the fans were perched on a narrow verge, behind which there was a small ditch, filled with ballast, and, beyond that, was the Voie Ferrée du Dauphiné, the tramline which ran between Grenoble and Bourg d'Oisons. Beyond the tramline was a steep drop into the ravine.

About one hundred metres from the bend, Prior also made a move and passed to the left of Paco, his legs pounding the pedals. Paco momentarily looked across at his friend and prepared to follow his wheel, but then, Le Grevès and Pélissier, were also moving through. He held his line and let the file of riders pass him. He was vaguely aware of the rumble of an engine from one of the following cars and he realised he was now at the back of the group. Paco fixed his attention on the rear wheel in front of him and leaned his bike into the right-hand bend. It was at that moment that disaster struck.

PART ONE

ROAD TO THE TOUR

1

VICTORY AND DEFEAT

Paco wiped the rain away from his eyes as he stood on the start line, preparing to race in the Championships of Biscay for a second time. He had finished fifth at the regional championships the previous year, at the age of just nineteen. It was a major breakthrough for such a young and inexperienced rider, but he was confident he could perform even better at the second attempt.

Long before Paco had ever heard about the Tour de France, he quickly earned a reputation for being an impetuous rider who would often go hell for leather from the start of a race in an effort to drop the field. His aggressive style of riding in his first year with his local club, the Sopuerta Sport Team, immediately brought him two victories, at Barakaldo and at the Circuito de Getxo race, before he impressed on his debut at the regional championships.

As he grew in confidence, Paco left his local club and joined the Athletic Club Cycling Team in Bilbao, the capital of the province of Biscay. At the time, the top football teams in Spain, like Real Madrid, had cycling and athletic teams attached to them. Paco's new team was linked with the Athletic

Bilbao Football Club and, as a result, had far more resources than Sopuerta Sport. With his new club, his winning streak continued, bringing him to where he now stood, hopeful of achieving his biggest ever victory. However, naivety leads to mistakes and, like all young riders, Paco was about to learn the highs and lows of bike racing the hard way.

There were twenty-two others alongside him on the morning of the fourth of October, as they set off from Campo Volantín and raced for ninety-seven kilometres in steady rain. At the beginning of a climb, in the town of Zugastieta, Paco made a blistering attack, which left his rivals gasping. Later in the race, he applied still more pressure, producing a series of similar bursts on the first ramps of the main climb. Towards the top of Erletxe, he found himself alone. Paco had a minute's advantage over four riders: Cesareo Sardis, Segundo Barruetabeña, Jesús García and Remigo Loroño.

Maintaining his advantage, Paco got to the foot of Enékuri. However, it was here that the young Basque rider was dealt his first harsh lesson. Already dreaming of riding across the finish line with his arms outstretched in the classic victory salute, Paco suddenly began to feel lightheaded and disorientated. He felt he was about to faint and fall, so he slowed dramatically until he came to a stop. It seemed as if the blood had been drained from his body and his legs felt weak. Paco gingerly climbed off his bike. Feeling unsteady, he sat down by the side of the road and put his head between his knees. Slowly, his head began to clear, and he suddenly remembered he was leading a bike race and was not far from the finish line. He swung his leg over his bike and started pedalling, feeling a rush of adrenalin from the fear of being caught by his pursuers. However, a little further along the road, to his frustration, the feelings of weakness and light-headedness returned. Paco was forced to stop for a second time. The road stretched out ahead of him and the victory he had visualised quickly evaporated.

He looked back down the road and, to his horror, he could see a cloud of dust, out of which the chasers appeared. They were less than two hundred metres away. His advantage had been slashed. His first major title, which had seemed within his grasp, now looked like it would be cruelly snatched from him.

When asked about it later, Paco could not recall exactly where it came from but, with a colossal effort, he managed to gather himself and stamp on the pedals as hard as he could towards the finish-line in Bilbao. He dared not look back. If he had, he would have seen his rivals breathing down his neck. Much better to look forward and hold his nerve. With his chin almost touching the handlebars, Paco summoned up every ounce of remaining energy in his body. He descended into the city on his own, crossing the finish line, and claiming his first Championship, with a twenty second advantage. Such was his relief on reaching the line that he completely forgot to raise his arms aloft in victory.

The first victory in a major event is always a special one, and Paco's was so dramatic it was one he would never forget. So many things had conspired against him; the weather had been cold and wet, sapping his energy, and his rivals had been dogged in their relentless pursuit. Worst of all, he had so nearly been the architect of his own downfall, by neglecting to eat enough during the race. It had been a painful lesson. In local races, his tactic of riding from the front had worked. But now he was competing at a higher level, against more experienced and hardened riders, he would have to learn to conserve his energy and sharpen his tactics. At the finish, he had to be helped from his bike. His customary smile had turned to a grimace. Pain and hunger wracked his body. It was not a good feeling and definitely one he was keen to avoid in future races.

Paco returned to Sopuerta after his victory where he was becoming something of a local hero. He had been born in this small, working-class, iron mining town, in the Basque region of

Spain, thirty-five kilometres from Bilbao, on the ninth of March 1906, to Augustín Cepeda and Tomasa Nistal. He was baptised Francisco Cepeda Nistal but to his family and friends he was always known as Paco or Paquito — 'Little Paco'. The family were originally from San Justo de la Vega, in León province, a small village near the historic town of Astorga. Augustín and Tomasa had moved to Sopuerta, at the end of the nineteenth century. Their eldest son, Gerardo, was born there on the twenty-sixth of September 1900 and Paco followed six years later. There were four other siblings; brothers, Primitivo, Gregorio and Fernando and a sister Espe. Paco's younger cousin, Teresa, also lived with the family. Times were hard at the beginning of the twentieth century and there were many mouths to feed so they were not wealthy.

The Cepeda family ran a small, general store in the heart of Sopuerta and the town relied on iron ore mining for its survival. Most of the teenage boys in the region around Sopuerta worked in the iron mines or the kilns, where the refining process started, but it was Paco's good fortunate to work in the store, alongside his father and mother. He was, by far, the happiest of the Cepeda brothers, always smiling, laughing and joking, and when he was given his freedom from the shop or the vegetable garden, Paco's face would light up. He would take his bike and head straight for the surrounding hills. To leave the confines of Sopuerta was pure joy. Each time he rode his bike, it felt like the beginning of new adventure, an escape to another world. Over time, as he grew stronger and bolder, his rides took him further and further from his town. Paco nearly always began his journeys by climbing Las Muñecas which overlooked Sopuerta. He had a very small but powerful frame which was well-suited to the undulating countryside around his home and, in these early years, he quickly developed the skills and stamina of a climber.

As Champion of Biscay, Paco had beaten some seasoned

amateurs, but he had also defeated some experienced professionals. Spanish professionals rarely raced abroad. Occasionally, they might travel across the Pyrenees and try their luck in a race in France, but mostly they stayed on home soil where they could earn a reasonable living if they were successful. Professionals from France, Belgium and Italy would contest some of the bigger road races in Spain and they came with stories about the biggest bicycle race in the world, the Tour de France. It was from these hardened men Paco first heard tales of epic mountain climbs in the Alps and Pyrenees and monumental stages of over four hundred kilometres. On his training rides, he began to dream about racing against the top European riders and, as he powered to the top of Las Muñecas, he imagined himself cresting one of the famous Alpine cols.

In the years that followed, Paco continued to grow his reputation as a strong and honest rider who never gave up, even when the odds were stacked against him. Throughout 1927, he continued to ride for the Athletic Club and firmly established himself as the best rider in Biscay, as well as making a name for himself nationally. His dream of riding against some of Europe's stars was realised sooner than he could have imagined when he rode his first Vuelta al País Vasco, a four stage race over seven hundred and seventy kilometres. Paco lined up against former Tour de France winners, Lucien Buysse from Belgium and Nicolas Frantz from Luxembourg, as well as the rising star from France, André Leducq. Leducq had won gold at the 1924 Paris Olympic Games. You might have imagined the young Cepeda would have been overawed riding in such elite company, but from the start of the race in Bilbao, Paco was in the thick of the action.

Stage one to Vitoria used many of the roads on which Paco regularly trained, including Las Muñecas. At four kilometres in length and six percent, it was a testing, punchy climb but, on this occasion, Paco would be descending it, into his home town. The race was passing his house in Sopuerta and he knew his family would be cheering and waving from the roadside. On the descent into Sopuerta, he planned to be at the head of the race, to give his family and friends a wave and a smile. Some early attacks, which Paco missed, threatened to wreck his plan but the international stars, known as the Aces, led by Frantz, came to his aid. By the time the peloton reached Sopuerta, at sixty-four kilometres, it had reeled in the early breakaway. Paco got his wish. The moment only lasted a matter of seconds, as the main field flashed through the sleepy town which basked in the peace and silence of the early morning sunshine, but it was a special moment for Paco. Riding shoulder to shoulder with two Tour de France giants, in front of his excited family and friends, was an amazing feeling. His grin was as wide as the Sopuerta valley. This proved to be the highlight of Paco's day. Leducq was victorious in Vitoria and although Paco faded towards the end of the stage, he still managed to finish thirteenth out of the thirty-nine starters.

On the second stage from Vitoria to Pamplona, Paco again rode magnificently. He climbed the rocky peaks of the Urbasa mountain range in thick fog, riding on the wheel of Buysse. He stuck with the French star for most of the day and finished only thirty-seven seconds in arrears of the former Tour winner. Leducq again dominated the day and won his second consecutive stage, but Paco finished tenth and jumped to ninth in the general classification. He was enjoying his first taste of international cycling, but on stage three, from Pamplona to San Sebastián, he was in for a rude awakening.

The race began on the outskirts of Pamplona and became a fierce battle between the two professional teams of Alcyon, led by Leducq, and Automoto, led by Lucien Buysse. Automoto were keen to isolate the leader Leducq, and in Buysse, Georges Ronsse, Alfred Haemerlinck, Jules Buysse and Joseph

Van Dam, they had the firepower to do it. Victor Fontan, who rode for Elvish-Wolber, was perfectly placed to take advantage. He had already won the Volta a Catalunya and, as he was racing alone, he sat at the back of the lead group, conserving his energy and devising his plan. Automoto's relentless pace of forty kilometres per hour, or more, for long periods, meant that Leducq was eventually dropped, along with Paco and Paco's fellow Spaniards, Ricardo Montero and Telmo Garcia. These four then worked hard together to bridge the gap back to the lead group, after crossing the border into France. By the time they had reached the foot of the Osquich, at one hundred and nineteen kilometres, they had rejoined the leaders, but it was just at that point Fontan, who had been quietly biding his time, attacked. He rode clear on the climb and descended faster than anyone, building up a sizeable lead. The fast start and the chase had taken its toll on Paco and, of the Spaniards, only Montero could respond. He crossed the summit in second place. Even Buysse was struggling, paying the price for his aggressive start. Paco had ridden bravely, but it was now a case of limiting his losses as the race passed through Bayonne, before heading back into Spain. In the end, Fontan had strength in reserve and, aided by punctures to Buysse and Montero, won the stage easily. Leducq had three punctures and rode much of the stage on his own. The two hundred and sixty-six kilometre stage had hurt everyone except Fontan. He finished almost twenty minutes ahead of Buysse, in second place, and took the overall lead from Leducq, who had a wretched day. Paco came home in eighteenth position, with the Peugeot rider, Julien Vervaecke, over an hour down on the stage winner. He dropped from ninth place to fifteenth in the general standings with one stage to go.

It had been an up and down race for Paco but he was optimistic he would have a good ride on the final stage to Bilbao, especially as he had been forced to ride conservatively on the second half of stage three.

'This is my stage,' he confidently told reporters on the morning of the race. 'We'll see. I'm going home.'

The stage would be a testing one. One hundred and seventy kilometres along the coastline, with a detour inland to take in the ascent of the Sollube, the Basque Tourmalet. The mountain rises to an elevation of six hundred and eighty-one metres and the road is eight and a half kilometres long, with an average gradient of over eight per cent. Fontan had identified the climb as the place where there could be an attack that would decide the race.

It was a beautiful morning, with many families enjoying themselves on San Sebastián's La Concha beach. The sea was calm and the sun glistened in the early morning light. To the riders it must have looked an idyllic scene, but what awaited them was far from idyllic. The coast road was peppered with short steep climbs and dangerous precipitous descents, with sudden, sharp curves. As the riders prepared for the start, bathers rushed from the beach and joined the human corridor of fans lining the streets to cheer on their heroes. In the early part of the stage, there were a few skirmishes which came to nothing. As Fontan had predicted, it was not until the Sollube, at about one hundred and thirty-five kilometres, that there was any drama. The leading riders, which included Paco, hit the bottom of the climb at a very fast pace. Montero led the way up the climb, with Fontan, Buysse, and Paco on his wheel. Leducq had been left behind, and as the gradients reached almost thirteen per cent, near the summit, Buysse crossed first with Paco second. It looked like Paco was going to deliver on his promise. As they descended towards Larrauri, they continued to extend their lead. First, Montero lost touch, when he stopped to change the gear on his back wheel, and then Fontan stopped to rearrange some broken spokes in his back wheel. With Bilbao almost in sight, Paco and Buysse had a clear lead. As the pair raced towards the finish at the Arenas Velodrome, for the first time, Paco actually thought he could win the stage. He felt a surge of exhilaration. He was riding alongside a former Tour de France champion and they were a kilometre clear of the chasers. To stand on top of the podium, ahead of Buysse and other stars of the great race, would be beyond Paco's wildest dreams. But then catastrophe. Paco felt his rear tyre softening. He continued for three kilometres until he was riding on the rim and he was losing touch with Buysse's back wheel. Dismounting, he quickly tried to tear the tubular from the rim but it was stuck fast. He wrestled with it and the minutes ticked away. After finally removing it, he then struggled to fit a new tubular. It was too tight. He desperately tried to stretch it but he was losing time. Three minutes passed, then four, and then five. His dream of winning the stage was in ruins. All he could do was cry out to the heavens, in agony. Several riders passed him before he finally fitted the tubular and pumped it up.

Buysse, Fontan and Haemerlinck, entered the packed velodrome together, completed two laps and then contested the sprint. Buysse deservedly won, but Fontan took the overall victory. Four minutes later, a thoroughly dejected Paco entered the arena in eleventh place. However, his spirits were immediately raised by the thunderous reception he received from the crowd of fourteen thousand, fanatical, Basque fans. They had been hearing announcements over the loud speaker system, giving them updates about the incidents in the latter stages of the race. As soon as he entered the stadium, the mass of spectators rose to its feet and clapped and cheered. Men and boys waved their caps, hats and berets in appreciation of their local hero and they did not stop once Paco crossed the line. They continued with their cheering, encouraging him to cycle a lap of honour. It was an emotional moment for Paco who felt like the victor. It had been a courageous ride and, despite the disappointment of not being able to challenge Buysse for the stage victory, Paco had the consolation of finishing thirteenth in the final classification and winning seven hundred pesetas.

Paco's stunning ride on the final stage, against some of the stars from the Tour de France, certainly turned a few heads. He was already a local celebrity but now foreign riders and reporters would also be talking about the rising Basque star, Francisco Cepeda.

That same year, Paco sought to expand his experience by competing in some track races. Paco loved them as they were fast and furious and they attracted very large crowds to the velodromes. He won the pursuit event with Segundo Barruetabeña, in Ibaiondo and, throughout April, the pair were undefeated. Standing out on the track, in spite of being mainly a road cyclist, proved that Paco was a truly versatile rider.

The Championships of Biscay once again closed the local racing season and Sopuerta's favourite son made the road race a race against the clock. On the muddy hill of Umbe, whilst his rivals struggled to keep their machines upright, their rear wheels spinning in the sloppy mud, Paco sat in his saddle and pedalled away from them. He had learned from his mistakes the previous year and was able to measure his effort perfectly. Overtaking Fernando Ibáñez, José Bereincua, Fédérico Ezquerra and Jesús Dermit, his lone adventure began. From there to the line, Paco worked hard for his second Championship victory, on this occasion winning not by seconds, but by five minutes over Dermit and Ezquerra.

Wanting to make the most of his form and fitness, he took part in the Spanish Championships, a one hundred kilometre time trial in Barcelona, at the end of October 1927. Paco was third, which reinforced the message that a new Basque talent was on the rise. Paco, however, was disappointed with his performance. His reaction showed how far he had come that year and increased his desire for further success.

He was now a celebrity in Sopuerta and famous throughout the province of Biscay but, the following year, his mandatory two-year military service was upon him, and he was forced to leave his beloved home and family and move to Madrid, where his regiment would be based. He left the Athletic Club and joined Real Madrid. Fortunately, because of his status as an up-and-coming cycling star, he was given time off by the army to train and race.

In April, he won the Gran Premio Pamplona and, for most of the summer, he continued his success, never finishing out of the top two in his races. His reputation as one of Spain's top riders was now firmly established but the Madrid papers were not always generous towards him. He was expected to win every race he entered and when he did not, he had to face the criticism from the media. However, his season came to a premature close when, in September 1928, his regiment received orders to deploy to Nador, in Morocco. Here, he spent eight months without his bike. It was torture for Paco not being able to ride. Each day he could feel his physical condition declining and he wondered whether he would ever be able to recapture the form he had shown the previous year.

Having spent the winter in Africa, he returned to Spain in May 1929. He started training again and quickly re-established his position in the hierarchy of Spanish cycling, finishing second in a race in Legazpi. He repeated the feat a week later in Beasain, being beaten on both occasions by his friend and rival Luciano Montero. On the second of June, Paco finally got his revenge, winning a race in Santander over sixty-five kilometres. Then, three weeks later, in the Campazar race, which covered over one hundred and four kilometres, Paco was victorious again. He broke from the rest of the field, within one kilometre of the port, and won in a sprint finish, once again against Montero.

Faithfully returning to the Championships of Biscay, Paco arrived in great spirits, excited to revive old glories and win the race for a third time. But there was a surprise, as it was not Dermit or Paco who took the victory, but Barruetabeña who won in a sprint. Paco had to settle for second again. By the end of the season, he had recorded six victories and five second places.

From humble beginnings, riding for his hometown cycling club in local road races, by 1930, Paco had become one of Spain's foremost riders. He had dominated his local races in the Basque Country and made a name for himself with his aggressive racing style. He had even gone toe to toe with some of best professional riders in Europe, including two former Tour de France winners. The thought of riding against Europe's elite riders no longer seemed so daunting and Paco's dream of riding in the toughest bike race of all, the Tour de France, seemed within touching distance. If he managed it, Paco would become only the second Basque cyclist to ride in the Tour de France. If he was to survive it, Paco would need to channel the remarkable strength and resilience of the man who paved the way — Vicente Blanco, otherwise known as 'El Cojo' or 'The Lame One'.

2

INDOMITABLE BASQUE SPIRIT

Vicente Blanco's life was tough from the very start. Born on the fifteenth of March 1884, in Bilbao, he was orphaned as a young child. He went to sea at the age of twelve, working as a cook. Ironically, it was during his years as a sailor that he discovered his passion for road cycling. Renting a bike, once he had arrived in the different ports of Europe, he explored his foreign surroundings, as well as developing his strength and skills as a cyclist. By the age of sixteen, tired of his life at sea, Vicente found work at the Basconia steelworks in Bilbao. It was while working there that he suffered the first of two serious accidents. At the Basconia factory, the upper part of his left foot was struck by a red-hot iron bar, almost completely disabling him. Then, when working at the Euskalduna shipyard, his right foot was caught in a gear. The foot was saved, but his toes had to be amputated. These workplaces were notorious for their filthy and dangerous working conditions and accidents were all too common, as Vicente found to his cost.

With the meagre compensation Vicente received from his employers, he purchased a small boat and became the ferryman on the Ria de Bilbao. He fished for eels to supplement his poor income and to avoid starvation. Despite his disability, his spirit and thirst for adventure remained undaunted. He tried swimming, rowing and then boxing, before finally turning back to the bike which had brought him so much happiness as a boy. He sold his boat and bought a bike for four pesetas which he then had to completely restore. Next, he began to train seriously, in the hope that he might be able to make a living from the one sport he truly loved.

However, it seemed impossible that a severely lame man of twenty-one could earn a living as a racing cyclist. When he approached the Basque Cycling Federation for a racing licence, they refused but, out of sympathy for his predicament, the Federation allowed him to take part in one of its races, in Bilbao. Initially looked upon by the spectators with a mixture of scorn and pity, Vicente amazed everyone by finishing second, beating more experienced athletes and defying those who had mocked and doubted him. He followed up this performance with a third place in the Grand Prix of Vitoria. The Federation no longer had a case against him so agreed to give him a full racing licence. By 1906, he had finished fourth in the Basque Championships and was beginning to attract the attention of sponsors. Armor, the bicycle manufacturer, offered him a basic sponsorship deal and gave him a better bike to ride.

Now known as 'the Lame One', a nickname which he was happy to accept, Vicente continued to astonish everyone with his performances. By 1908, he had finished runner up in the Basque Championships and proudly represented the Basque region in the Spanish Championships. Too poor to pay for his travel to Gijon, Vicente rode the two hundred and sixty-five kilometres along the northern coastline to take his position on the start line. His heroic spirit could not be defeated, and he

stormed to victory in a sprint finish ahead of Esteban
Espinoza, despite crashing thirty kilometres from the finish.
Vicente still had not done enough to win over the Spanish
cycling fans but he had won a place in the hearts of the Basque
people. His victory meant he could afford to return to Bilbao
by rail and he received a hero's welcome when his train pulled
into the station. At a reception given to him by the Basque
Cycling Federation, he waved to crowds from the balcony but
was almost lost for words. All he could manage was a simple
sentence.

'I cannot speak,' he said. 'But I can ride a bike.'

The crowds cheered loudly.

It seemed Vicente could do no wrong in the eyes of his
adoring Basque fans, but despite his victory in Madrid-Toledo-
Madrid, at the start of the 1909 season, Spanish fans
continued to doubt him. Keen to prove his first national championship was no fluke, he returned to defend his title. During
the race, the former winner and two-time champion of Spain,
José Luis Amuñategui, who had been banned the previous year,
approached Vicente and offered him five hundred pesetas to let
him win. This was not uncommon in professional cycling and,
whether right or wrong, Vicente, who was always short of
money, accepted. However, that was not the end of it. A third
rider, Juan Peñalba, got wind of the agreement and made it
clear he intended to beat them both. Amuñategui, not wanting
Pealba to win, gave Vicente the freedom to attack, which he
did, finishing thirty-four minutes ahead of his two rivals. He
covered the final hundred kilometres at an average speed of
twenty-five kilometres an hour. A few critics remained, but they
were finally silenced when he later rode to victory in the classic
race, Irun-Pamplona-Irun.

Ungainly and awkward when he walked, once sitting
astride his Amor bicycle, it was as if Vicente was grafted to his

machine. He rode with such elegance and efficiency that his disability completely vanished.

Now firmly accepted as Spain's best rider, Manuel Aranaz, the President of the Basque Federation, suggested Vicente register for the 1910 Tour de France. He leapt at the chance, even though he did not have enough funds to transport himself and his bike to Paris. There was also the announcement that the eighth edition of the Tour would visit the high mountains of the Pyrenees on the Luchon to Bayonne stage. In a single stage, *L'Auto* revealed, the riders would climb the Peyresourde, Aspin, Tourmalet, Soulor and Aubisque passes. This revelation came from Henri Desgrange, the director of the Tour de France, and it prompted a quarter of the riders, who had already registered, to withdraw before the start of the race. Giving up never entered Vicente's mind. Once he had set his mind on something, he approached the challenge with a supernatural strength.

Four days before the start of the race, Vicente set out from Bilbao on an incredible one thousand, one hundred kilometre ride to Paris. He arrived on the eve of the race with barely enough time to visit the offices of *L'Auto* where he picked up his race number and a bike loaned to him by Alcyon Cycles. In the early hours of the next morning, he was on the start line alongside the greatest riders of the time, Octave Lapize, François Faber, Gustave Garrigou and Henri Cornet.

Sadly, human endurance has its limits, and this was the closest Vicente would ever get to these cycling greats. Exhausted from his superhuman efforts getting to Paris, he was soon dropped by the peloton on the opening stage. He raced alone for two hundred kilometres, suffering terrible hunger, as well as several falls and various mechanical problems. Riding without food and on unfamiliar roads, Vicente's formidable spirit was pushed to its very limits. No one would have blamed him for quitting, but suffering had become a way of life to

Vicente Blanco. Quitting was not an option. This man had more scars on his body than all the Spanish bullfighters combined, according to the famous bullfighter, Cocherito de Bilbao. And so, Vicente somehow completed that first stage, arriving in Roubaix an isolated figure, long after the other riders had finished. Undeterred, Vicente was determined to start the second stage the following morning but, sadly, the organisers had other ideas. He had finished outside the time limit and he had to be eliminated. The rules stated that riders had to finish the stage in a time which was within eight per cent of the winner's time. Desgrange, who made the rules, was not a sentimental man. The rules were the rules. It was as simple as that.

Considering himself to be a failure, Vicente was keen to keep as low a profile as possible on his return to Bilbao. He need not have worried. At Bilbao station, he was greeted by a huge crowd. A Spaniard competing in the Tour de France. What could be more remarkable than that? And to think, he had undertaken that formidable ride to Paris just to get to the start line. Now known throughout Spain and abroad, Vicente was rewarded with a two year contract with the famous French cycle manufacturer Alcyon.

Vicente and Paco had much in common. Both had a genuine love of the bike and a sense of adventure. They used their bikes to break free from the narrow confines in which they lived, to explore the world around them. In races, they were courageous and fiercely committed and, when faced with setbacks, they drew on that unbreakable Basque spirit. Like Vicente, Paco was on a path to becoming one of Spain's best riders and he too would soon get his chance to make his homeland proud at the greatest race of all.

3

GALIBIER GLORY: THE 1930 TOUR DE FRANCE

By the 1930s, professional cycling had come a long way since the first decade of the twentieth century when Vicente Blanco was trying to scrape a living. The Tour de France was now big business and when National teams were introduced to the Tour de France in 1930, and an invitation was sent to the Spanish Federation, Paco was hoping to be included in the Spanish National team of eight riders.

At the beginning of the season, he had signed for the Cycling Club Soriano and was being coached by Eusebio Soriano. Eusebio was a former rider who now owned a bike shop and had set up his own cycling team. It was to be Paco's best year as a professional cyclist. He was now ranked in the top five Spanish riders and was the second best climber, after Vicente Trueba. When the team was announced, it was no surprise Paco was included. The twenty-four-year-old from Sopuerta joined Salvador Cardona, José Trueba, Valeriano Riera, Vicente Trueba, Juan Mateu, Jesús Dermit and Nicolás Tubau in the first Spanish team to ride in the Tour de France.

Henri Desgrange, 'The Father of the Tour', was an uncompromising character who had been at odds with manufacturers, riders and rival newspaper reporters for years. He took the decision to move from manufacturers' teams to national teams, because he believed his race would be purer and the strongest rider would win. Since the first Tour in 1903, Desgrange was convinced rivalries between the manufacturers' teams had encouraged cheating. The best rider did not always win in Paris because a team could protect a chosen rider who otherwise might have struggled.

The best example was the Belgian, Maurice De Waele who won in 1929. He took the race lead after Victor Fontan crashed, in the pitch dark, and broke the front forks on his bike, eight kilometres into the stage. As no mechanical assistance was allowed and, at the time of the crash, all the race judges were ahead of the race, Fontan had to knock on every door in a nearby village before he found someone who would lend him a bike. The bike was too small for him but, nevertheless, he rode on with his broken bike strapped to his back. Desgrange's draconian rules stipulated that a rider could use a replacement bike but had to prove to the race judges, at the end of the stage, that the bike he had started on was beyond repair. Fontan continued for one hundred and forty-four kilometres but was an hour behind the race leaders. The broken bike was digging into his back and he was in unbearable pain. Unsurprisingly, he finally abandoned in tears.

De Weale, now in the yellow jersey, then became ill in Grenoble before the Galibier stage and had to be pushed and dragged over the mountains by his Alcyon teammates. The team blocked the road to deter attacks from rival teams and made alliances with other teams and individuals in an attempt to protect De Weale. Alcyon teammate, Marcel Bidot, admitted that he had prevented Benoît Faure from attacking by holding onto his saddle and the Belgian, Jef Deymursere, who was riding in his first Tour for a rival team, admitted making an alliance with Alcyon, to help his countryman hang onto the yellow jersey until the finish line in Paris. Deymursere finished second but was later demoted to third by Desgrange.

Desgrange was furious because he thought De Weale had only won the race with help from his team. His comment, 'the Tour has hit rock bottom. We have a corpse for a winner,' summed up his disgust.

Desgrange's changes to the race format in 1930 were not only because he wanted more control over the teams and the riders, he was also concerned that the race was becoming more predictable with it being dominated by teams like Alcyon, Automoto and Peugeot. Having built up a sizeable media following and international fanbase, he was worried French fans would lose interest in the race. Since 1923, there had been a string of victories by foreign riders, much to the frustration of the French public. The French had potential winners in Antonin Magne, Leducq and Bidot, but the manufacturers' teams preferred foreign riders as their team leaders. With a new set of rules, and all the riders under contract to *L'Auto*, Desgrange would now have complete control over the riders and the race, with the power to hand out punishments to any riders who broke his rules. Desgrange's hope was, with eight of the top riders from each of the leading cycling nations in Europe competing, any one of them had the potential to win the race. He assumed that every rider would be striving to win the race, but the reality was it was more likely that the national teams would appoint a captain and the remaining seven riders would ride for him, in much the same way as the riders in the commercial teams had sacrificed their chances for their leader.

This was the new-look Tour Paco and his Spanish team-mates prepared to take on. It would be a major challenge for the Spanish riders, many of whom were debutants who were unaccustomed to racing abroad. The Spanish also had the added disadvantage of having to ride the very basic production line bikes *L'Auto* had provided. This was another measure intro-

duced by Desgrange to limit the influence of the manufacturers. The same bike would be provided to every rider. It would
be painted yellow, to match the colour of his newspaper, *L'Auto*,
and display the name of the newspaper. Desgrange kept the
identity of the manufacturer of the bike secret. However, even
this would be open to abuse. Rumours circulated that the
better, and more famous riders, the Aces, had brought their
own bikes, provided by their sponsors, like Alcyon, and then
disguised them by painting them in the yellow livery of the
organisation.

Despite the huge challenges provided by the world's
toughest bike race, Paco equipped himself magnificently in his
debut Tour, especially in the mountains, on the Aubisque, the
Tourmalet and the Allos. However, it was on the famous Galibier where Paco emphatically introduced himself to the Tour
de France.

Monday 21st July 1930, Stage 16, Grenoble to Evian, 331kms

Sixty-three riders left Grenoble on route to Evian, at three
o'clock in the morning. They faced three hundred and
thirty-one of the most brutal kilometres. Paco had begun to
find his climbing legs on the previous stage, a three hundred
and thirty-three kilometre alpine leg from Nice to Grenoble,
when he had finished in twelfth place. He had been grateful for
the rest day in Grenoble, knowing that the biggest challenge of
his racing life lay ahead of him.

The start of the day was unusually cold. The riders were
up at one o'clock in the morning for breakfast and signing on
at two o'clock. Despite the early start, there was still a healthy
crowd gathered around the signing-on table. On the start line,

to combat the cold, many riders covered their muscular thighs with black silk stockings and their arms with white cotton stockings. Litres of boiling juice were available to warm their shivering bodies. That morning, the peloton crawled out of Grenoble at a snail's pace, in the pitch black. Only the headlights of the following convoy of cars illuminated the road. The breeze seemed even cooler on their faces as they eased along. The night sky, dotted with a mass of tiny sparkling stars, watched the peloton as it snaked its way slowly towards the mountains.

No one was eager to break away and who could blame them with hours of hard riding ahead of them. In the gloom of the early morning, the riders even had time to admire the stunning town of Vizelle, the birthplace of the French Revolution. Little by little, the darkness lifted and the smoking and glowing factories of the Oisan valley began to reveal themselves. The river torrents roared beside the riders and a smoky-ice drizzle occasionally enveloped them.

Between Bourg d'Oisans and La Grave, a magnificent spectacle began to slowly emerge. The Meije Massif, with its eternal snows and massive blue glaciers came into view. Even those riders who were now beginning to toil against the gradually steepening gradient could not resist lifting their heads occasionally, from their front wheels, to steal a glance at this magnificent natural wonder. The mountain tops were covered in snow and had a wintry look, but as the rising sun lightly touched the peaks, it coloured them in a redness which then descended slowly along the mountain sides, dissolving into a pinky white. Then, as the sun rose higher, it seemed to illuminate the whiteness of the Meije.

As the bodies of the riders began to warm with their effort, many of them began to discard their leggings. And, so, eventually, with no significant attacks, the riders first approached the Col du Lautaret, the gateway to the Galibier. Paco felt like they could not have ridden at more than fifteen kilometres per hour until they arrived at La Grave. Then, with seventy-six kilometres covered, the fancied riders began to push a little harder, as the road continued to climb slowly and surely towards what was the first col of the day. It was on this steady but punishing drag that gaps gradually began to open.

By the time Paco had reached the col, which stands at two thousand and fifty-eight metres, he could see the backs of Leducq, Learco Guerra and Jef Demuysere moving a slight distance ahead. At the summit of the col, with the majestic and imposing glaciers to their right, they headed downhill, for a couple of kilometres, in the direction of Briançon, before swinging left and turning almost one hundred and eighty degrees to begin their ascent of the Galibier. At this hairpin, several of the riders, including Paco, dismounted to take advantage of a smaller gear, by removing and flipping their back wheels. André Leducq, the yellow jersey sitting proudly on his shoulders, was the exception. He kept going, slowly turning a bigger gear. Barely one hundred kilometres had been covered.

The road was nothing more than a dusty, gravel track. The going was tough and it would steadily get tougher. Once Paco started climbing again, with his teammate Trueba in close attendance, he could see Leducq's yellow jersey ahead, but he tried not to close the gap immediately, preferring to concentrate on keeping a smooth pedalling rhythm. Leducq was clearly working extremely hard to establish a gap between himself and his pursuers. If he could open a sizeable lead, then there was a chance those behind might be less inclined to chase. Paco briefly saw the overall race leader stretch his lead to about thirty metres on Guerra and Demuysere. But this was not a decisive enough break. The invisible elastic between leader and pursuers had not been broken and now Leducq seemed to be labouring against the incline and the high gear that he was still turning. When Paco next looked up, Leducq had finally dismounted to change his gears. With that, the gap was rapidly closed.

Benoît Faure eased past Paco and Trueba, but the two Spaniards were unfazed and continued to tap out a regular rhythm. Paco was content to ride his own race. For now, he felt in control but, on a long climb like the Galibier, that feeling could change in an instant and there was no telling when. One thing was guaranteed, if he pushed too hard, he might awaken that feeling of numbness and fatigue, so, for now, he was happy to hold back. In contrast, Faure was making a huge effort and was soon passing Guerra and then Demuysere. Five hundred metres into the climb, Paco saw Leducq beginning to falter for the first time, which gave him hope. The yellow jersey, the leader of the Tour, was now being caught and passed by Benoît Faure, and now Pierre Magne had entered the battle, appearing on Paco's shoulder. With half of the mighty Galibier conquered, the race was on and Paco was filled with renewed energy. Other riders were strung out in ones and twos down the mountain side, toiling against the vicious slope. They were clearly visible against the barren, rock-strewn landscape. Paco was challenging the greatest riders in the world, on the Tour's most brutal mountain. His adrenalin was pumping.

There was an extraordinary crowd of people lining the mountain road as the stony track headed towards the tunnel, near the summit. This was the moment that he had long dreamed of as a young cyclist. Leducq had overreached himself and was now coming back to them with every turn of the pedals. What a moment it was, as the two Spanish riders, in their red and yellow bands, passed the Frenchman in his yellow jersey. Paco remembered looking across at Leducq. He smiled at the race leader who, with drawn eyes, simply nodded in acknowledgment. But Paco was now focusing on Guerra, who was also in trouble, and on Demuysere who, similarly, was falling back. Meanwhile higher up, Pierre Magne moved easily and powerfully and he had caught the leader, Benoît Faure. Locked together, these two entered the tunnel and crested the Galibier in first place. As Paco approached the summit, he passed, and immediately dropped, a tiring Guerra. Ahead, Demuysere's lone figure plunged into the darkness of the tunnel, less than one hundred metres ahead of the Spanish duo.

The Giant of the Alps, standing at two thousand five hundred and seventy-six metres had been conquered and Paco had crossed the col in fourth place. His teammate Trueba, whom he had paced up the mountain was on his shoulder. It was eight-sixteen when the pair emerged from the cool blackness of the tunnel on the Maurienne side, into the bright, crisp, morning sunshine. They were a mere fifty-five seconds behind Faure and Magne, and Demuysere's rear wheel was in touching distance. The great Leducq and Guerra were twenty-five seconds back. Behind them, the rest of the field had been destroyed and was strung out as far as the Col du Lautaret. The great Charles Pélissier was over nine minutes in arrears.

Paco sat up and took a moment to savour his triumph. Whatever happened now, nobody could take this away from him. But there is hardly a moment for a rider in the Tour de France to take his eye from the road. This is especially true in the mountains, where the road surfaces were nothing more than loose gravel, flint and stone. Every turn of the road screamed danger. It was so easy to misjudge a bend and for the bike to slide and the rider to fall. Paco was so focused he had no time to notice Chocolat-Menier, the first sponsor to sign up for Desgrange's new publicity caravan, had not set up their usual drinks station, where cups of hot chocolate would be handed out to riders as they crested the col. Often they would camp out overnight on the mountain tops but, even though the Galibier had been overrun with spectators, representatives from Menier were nowhere to be seen. In spite of its absence, the first five riders would each take a share of the five thousand francs prime, the seventh prime of the race offered by the Chocolate maker. But Paco had more important matters to attend to than hot chocolate or prize money.

Paco never thought of himself as a great descender. He was nowhere near the slowest but he was nowhere near the fastest either. It was not that he was afraid. He simply did not see the point in taking unnecessary risks. Better to lose a minute or two on the long descent, than crash and damage the bike beyond repair, or worse, suffer an injury and be out of the race and fail to reach Paris.

The slopes that surrounded the Galibier were covered with large patches of snow. It was a beautiful sight and provided Paco with a magnificent view as he followed Trueba down the long, steep descent towards Valloire. Within a few minutes of crossing the col, Leducq sped past him like a madman. For the Frenchman, victory was at stake and he was prepared to throw caution to the wind. After negotiating the twists and turns below the tunnel, the leaders plummeted down the mountain towards Plan Lachet, where there was a brief respite, before the road steepened again towards the hamlets of Bonnenuit and Les Verneys. Leducq was quickly out of sight. Good luck to him thought Paco. He can follow his dream and I will follow mine. The descent of the Galibier is fast and dangerous but, once through Valloire, the road begins to climb again towards the fort, at the Col du Télégraphe, and on this short incline, Paco felt at home again. But then he was dropping like a stone for fifteen kilometres to the Maurienne valley floor and the town of Saint Michel.

However, the drama was not over for the day. As Paco rounded one of the many tight bends on the Télégraphe, there, sitting in a ditch, was Leducq, with his head in his hands and his knees badly bloodied. His teammate Pierre Magne, who had looked so impressive crossing the Galibier, was now holding Leducq's bike, with a look of exasperation on his face. Paco flashed past realising that Leducq had taken a bad fall and Magne had stopped to help him, but the distraction was brief. As fond as he was of Leducq, and he had no desire to see another rider suffer, he had no time to lose and he had no wish to end up like Leducq. Paco was now even more relieved that he had chosen caution, even though he had now lost contact with Trueba. He was somewhere up ahead, forming a leading pack with Demuysere, Guerra and Benoît Faure.

At nine forty-five, at the foot of the Télégraphe, Paco swung left into the town of Saint Michel and was grateful to stretch his back and find his rhythm again as the road finally flattened through the Maurienne valley. The road would wind its way along the narrow valley and gently descend all the way to Albertville. Paco was happy when he was joined by Louis De Lannoy, Georges Laloup, Adolf Schön and Oskar Tierbach. Fellow Spaniard, Vicente Trueba, had descended like an eagle and passed through Saint Michel four minutes earlier. He had a slight lead on Faure, Demuysere and Guerra.

As Paco now settled into his accustomed smooth pedalling pattern, following Laloup's wheel, he could not help thinking back to that moment when he led Trueba up the Galibier. What a moment for the Spanish team. He felt another surge of pride. His family and friends back in Sopuerta and Bilbao would soon hear of their incredible ride and the newspapers would write about their heroic efforts. But then his thoughts returned again to poor Leducq. Would his Tour be over? Paco did not have to wait long for this question to be answered.

At the end of the stage, even the French journalists would talk and write about the courage of the Spanish on the Galibier, but it was André Leducq who would make the headlines. When he had fallen on the Télégraphe, apart from suffering the usual grazes and cuts to his legs and elbows, he had also broken his pedal, which was more of a problem. Magne and Bidot had tried, in vain, to fix it and, when Paco had passed Leducq, sitting in the ditch, the race leader was bemoaning his bad luck. He believed he had lost the Tour de France. But then Leducq's luck changed. A railway worker, who had travelled from Modane to watch the race, appeared with a spanner, and a local boy, who had propped his bicycle against a tree, was more than happy to part with a pedal in exchange for Leducq's broken one. By now, practically the whole French team had arrived to support their leader and Jules Merviel removed the badly damaged pedal. The mood suddenly changed and, to cheers from the locals who had gathered to watch the drama unfold, the yellow jersey was soon on its way again.

What followed was an amazing chase. At Saint Michel, even though Paco had been delayed by a puncture, his small group had a nine-minute lead on Leducq's group. Trueba, in his group of four, was thirteen minutes and thirteen seconds ahead of the yellow jersey. Guerra, the Italian champion, was in Trueba's group and in second place in the overall classification, so there was a real possibility that Leducq could lose the yellow jersey. However, by Albertville, Leducq and his French team almost had the leaders in their sights. Bidot, Pélissier, the French captain, and the Mange brothers, Pierre and Antonin, had paced Leducq back into contention, riding superbly, each taking turns at the front.

In spite of the fact that strong headwinds blew through the Maurienne valley, the leading group of four still managed speeds of forty kilometres per hour. However, they took long turns on the front, sometimes working for two kilometres at a time. Demuysere was also reluctant to take his turn on the front and did not feel inclined to help. The Italian, Guerra, nicknamed 'the locomotive', was running out of steam. Meanwhile, behind, the French peloton was moving at hurricane speeds of up to fifty kilometres per hour. Twenty-two kilometres from Saint Michel, the gap had closed from thirteen minutes to eight minutes. Twelve kilometres later, in Épierre, it was down to seven minutes. Fifteen kilometres later, in Pont-d'Aiton, it was down to six minutes and fifteen kilometres from Albertville, it was down to three minutes and thirty seconds. The French express train had picked up other riders along the way, some of whom had been able to hang on, so the group was growing in size. What a surprise Paco had when Leducq's peloton steamed past him on the outskirts of Albertville. A hunting pack, led by four blue jerseys and one yellow. Pélissier was on the front, blowing through gritted teeth, his jaw jutting out over his handlebars, his eyes firmly fixed forwards, locked on the long straight road ahead. The head cold he had been complaining about that morning had been forgotten and Antonin Magne played his role, despite suffering terribly with saddle boils. With dark storm clouds gathering, two kilometres after Albertville, the gap to the four leaders was bridged and an unlikely and remarkable recovery had been completed. With two hundred and twenty-six kilometres covered, the French team had put up an incredible chase of around seventy five-kilometres; their sole goal was to keep Leducq in yellow.

After such a struggle, the chasers, and those caught, granted themselves a temporary truce. The peloton of twenty-two cruised up the rough Arly gorges and refuelled at Flumet. There was still the matter of the Aravis to be climbed. At only one thousand four hundred and seventy metres, it was no Galibier but, for the riders, having already covered nearly two hundred and fifty gruelling kilometres, and with heavy rain now falling, it was no small matter. The twenty-two, which included Paco, stayed together until near the top when Pélissier went on the attack and led Marcel Mazeyrat, De Lannoy, Paul Delbart, Pierre Magne, Guerra and Leducq over the col. Miraculously, it suddenly stopped raining, so that, on the descent, this group was able to open up a two hundred metre gap on Paco, Trueba and Antonin Magne, among others. Paco never gave up hope of catching the bullet train which was being driven on by Pélissier and had now passed through Bonneville, at two hundred and seventy-one kilometres. It was now two-thirty in the afternoon and they had been on the road for an agonising eleven and a half hours. Paco thought that the lead group must be tiring after their long, tough chase. His own legs seemed to be turning as if by themselves and his weary and swollen eyes seemed mesmerised by the cracks in the road and the grit which rushed beneath him. His shoulders and neck ached. Occasionally, he raised his tired head in the hope of seeing a rider ahead who might give his group something to work towards.

At Thonon, the storm returned and, as if the riders had not suffered enough, they were soaked again. Suddenly, to Paco's surprise, like some kind of mirage, through the road spray, he saw the lead group ambling along as if they were out on a gentle, Sunday club run.

As the day had started, at snail's pace, so it finished. By the time they reached the outskirts of Evian, their number had swelled to thirty. Vicente and José Trueba were both there, in what was proving to be an excellent day for the Spaniards. Paco found himself towards the front of the group, as the riders entered the finishing straight. They were greeted by a line of umbrellas. The crowd had stoically stayed to greet them, even though the finishing banner had been blown away by the wind.

For a moment, Paco thought about making a challenge. He tightened his grip on his handlebars and prepared to raise his weary body out of the saddle for the sprint. Sadly, his mind was no longer in command of his body and, anyway, sprinting was not his speciality. In the end, Leducq and Pélissier contested the sprint which, naturally, Leducq won. Paco did not have their speed but was given the same finishing time as

the winner. Three hundred and thirty-one kilometres in thirteen hours thirty-nine minutes and twenty-three seconds. In
the results, he appeared in fifteenth place as, in mass sprints,
the riders were classified in the same order as their race
numbers. The Spanish riders were on their limit, riding
distances of over three hundred kilometres in one stage. To do
so on such a monstrous stage demonstrated their plucky spirit.
No sooner had the lead group finished, the storm returned and
the crowd scattered for shelter. The remainder of the field
finished in ones and twos, bedraggled. Many were well outside
the time deadline.

By this time, Paco was already heading for the warm showers. After two Alpine stages, how he would enjoy his rest day in
Evian. He had not had his cup of hot chocolate at the top of
the Galibier but his efforts had earned him one thousand
francs, courtesy of Chocolat-Menier. He could add to this, one
hundred francs for his placing in the sprint and one hundred
and twenty francs for the Spanish team's placing on the stage.
It had been a great day.

Paco reflected on how far he had come since his days riding
as a junior for his local club, in road races around Biscay. The
foundations of his storming ride on the Galibier had been laid
on the hills around Sopuerta. Climbing Las Muñecas day after
day, summer and winter, in the rain and wind and the biting
cold, had perfected his skills as a climber; his strength and
endurance, his smooth pedalling style and an ability to dance
on the pedals when the gradient steepened. His dogged determination in the face of heartbreaking setbacks and his honest
endeavour had prepared him for this day. His dream of challenging the best riders in the world, in the Tour de France, the
greatest race in the world, had been fulfilled and he loved it.

L'Auto declared that Francisco Cepeda was the new Spanish
star. It reported that the little Basque man was, 'a delightful
boy and extremely interesting.' His race to the top of the Gali-

bier, on what was such a painful stage, was extraordinary for a racer in his first Tour. In a similar vein, *L'Intransigeant* commented that Paco had stood out as, 'one of the best climbers on the Galibier, confirming the promise that he had shown in previous races with his excellent pedalling technique.' He was described as, 'a magnificent racer who sprints easily on the final slopes of climbs with an impressive style.' Paco went on to finish twenty-seventh in his first Tour de France. In doing so, he became the first Basque rider to finish the race in Paris.

It was a remarkable achievement for such a young man. Paco had caught the eye of the organisers of the Tour, identifying him as an honest rider, who would be worthy of being invited back in future years to compete as an individual rider, if he had not already been chosen to ride for the Spanish National team. The following year he would be offered the chance to repeat his success. But Paco's next experience of the Tour de France would not be so enjoyable.

4

PAIN AND SUFFERING: THE 1931 TOUR DE FRANCE

I n March 1931, Paco, Ezquerra, Montero and Cañardo were invited by the French to race the five kilometre climb up Mont Faron, the mountain which dominated Toulon. It was a short, zig zag climb, with gradients rising to fourteen per cent. Fifty thousand fans turned up to watch. The climb was well-suited to Paco as it was very similar to the punchy climbs in the Basque Country where he trained. On his first visit to the race, he finished third and his name came to even greater prominence in French racing circles. He might have performed even better, with a little more shrewdness, but he missed his chance owing to a lapse in concentration. One hundred and twenty-six of the world's finest riders started that race and, in the closing stages, there were only two riders ahead of Paco but, naively, he thought there was a much larger group ahead of him. The mountain road was lined with spectators and it was hard to see anything ahead, other than a sea of faces. Paco knew he was in a great position but he had given up any hopes of victory. He could not understand why the fans were shouting at him and giving him so much support, urging him to ride faster. Had it not been for this error of judgement, he might have won the race or, at the very least, caught up with Pierre Pastorelli who was just ahead of him. As it was, he did not even contest the sprint for second place, thinking that several others had already crossed the finish line before him.

That summer, just as Paco was making an impact on the international scene, he was plagued with bad luck. He suffered from several falls, mistakes and missed opportunities and those close to him might have been forgiven for thinking he was cursed. It seemed he would also miss out on a return to the Tour de France, as the Spanish Federation was at loggerheads with the Tour organisation over the financial package they had been offered. Paco was desperate to represent Spain again at the Tour, spurred on by his excellent placing the previous year. For Paco, money was not the main motivation for riding the Tour, so a compromise was found and he set out for Paris as the only Spanish national team rider in the international field. However, riding as the sole member of the Spanish team presented Paco with a number of new challenges. He was isolated and unsupported and forced to make alliances with riders from other national teams. As an Ace, he received some mechanical support but essentially he felt like he was riding as an individual or touriste-routier. His first Tour had been like a dream but the second quickly turned into a nightmare.

In the opening stages, he had punctures, broke a pinion and he suffered terribly on the two hundred and six kilometre, third stage, from Dinan to Brest. He trailed home second to last, alongside the Australian, Ossie Nicholson, forty minutes down on the stage winner. Bravely, he rallied the following day to finish forty-fifth on the stage from Brest to Vannes. On stage five, from Vannes to Les Sables-d'Olonne, he finished with the main field, in thirty-fifth place, in a bunch sprint won by the master of the sprint, Pélissier. The next day's stage, to Bordeaux, was the longest of the race.

The riders spent nearly eleven hours in the saddle, tracing a line along the west coast of France, covering three hundred and thirty-eight kilometres. Paco suffered horribly again but he still managed a battling thirty-fifth place, only seven minutes and fifty-seven seconds behind the stage winner, Germany's Alfred Haemerlinck.

To a reporter, from the *Gazette de Biarritz*, who interviewed him at the end of the stage, Paco appeared a ghost-like figure. Looking at his frail frame, the journalist could not believe that Paco had completed so many stages of the Tour.

'Can you continue?' asked the reporter. 'Are you going to abandon?'

'I said that when this formidable task began, I did not think that I would be able to complete more than half the race,' Paco began. 'In the first place my form was bad and also, riding alone, and in difficult conditions, has not helped. However, the thought of leaving the race really hurts. That is why I have made every effort not to abandon and will continue racing.'

'How much longer can you keep going?'

'I must continue until my physical problems force me to surrender,' replied Paco. 'In the condition that I have ridden the Tour, it has been impossible for me to achieve worthwhile results and I have suffered horribly. This year, the Tour has been very hard. The team spirit amongst the national teams has dominated and I am racing alone, terribly alone. I feel even more isolated than the riders who race as individuals. When this is over, I plan to take a long rest in my Biscayan homeland.'

Paco finished the interview by insisting he would never ride the Tour again.

'I will not dispute the Tour again.' he said. 'However, I do not think that it is as fearsome as many people think. A Spanish team that has been well prepared, physically and morally, and with good advisers, has the potential to aspire to second or perhaps even first place.'

These words sounded like the words of a man close to accepting defeat. Yet, Paco battled on for thirteen more stages. He struggled over the Pyrenees, and he slogged over the Alps, determined to drag his tired and sick body to Paris. Ironically, in the end, he did not succumb to the pain or mental fatigue on the high mountain cols but on the flat roads of Alsace. On stage twenty, from Belfort to Colmar, with only four stages remaining before the grand finish in Paris, Paco's body and mind finally crumbled.

About twenty kilometres from the start in Belfort, Yves Dautin, a reporter with *Le Petit Parisien*, saw a rider sitting by the side of the road. He stopped his car. Paco was in floods of tears, so much so, that his body must have been wrung dry. His arms were wrapped around his stomach, his head was bowed between his knees, and he was softly moaning. Yves approached him.

'What is it?'

'The stomach! The stomach! Oh! There! It's very bad...All night...Hot sponges... I haven't slept...I haven't eaten this morning.'

'You are not going to abandon,' Yves replied, trying to encourage the spectral figure of Paco.

'I'm too ill,' groaned Paco.

The stabbing pains were unbearable at times but, in his mind, Paco was also thinking about Spain and those Spanish fans who would be following his progress. He was representing Spain. He alone was the Spanish team. Back in Sopuerta and Bilbao, he knew they would be urging him on and willing him to finish the race in Paris.

The Italian, Eugenio Gestri, another victim of sickness and fate, came to a halt beside them. Moved by Paco's distress, he smiled sweetly and offered Paco his hand.

'Come with me little Paco. Let's give it one more try.'

Gestri and Dautin helped Paco to his feet, and he painfully remounted his bike, grimacing. The two men rode on, slowly and weakly. They were united in their misery.

Sixty-two kilometres later, at the town of Altkirch, they could go no further and, finally, had to admit defeat. They climbed off their bikes. It had been a heroic effort. The Tour is conquered with the head and the legs but mostly with the stomach. When the stomach is not right, then it is over. More than the steepest cols or the burning heat of the sun, the riders fear the colic the most. The surrender came on a day when the roads were smooth. They cut deep into the fir forests which were bordered by beautiful, blue-black lakes and the sun shone brightly, turning the fields emerald green.

However, for Paco, it was a day of true suffering, a day from which he thought he would never recover. In contrast, the winner of the day's two hundred and nine kilometre stage to Colmar, André Leducq, commented, 'Today I was in a good mood. I felt like a tourist.' But he said it without his usual smile.

Paco returned to Spain after the Tour. When he had recovered from his illness, he took part in several national races, but the press was very tough on him and this shook his confidence. There were suggestions he was weak, that he could not adapt to racing abroad and he was too easily satisfied with finishing second. The press did not hold back and claimed he had become a real dandy, always dressing in the latest fashions. In short, he was accused of not taking his cycling seriously. Paco found these comments especially hurtful. He was young and single and fun loving but, once he was on his bike, he always trained as hard as he could. If the 1931 Tour proved anything, it was that Paco had a strong and indomitable spirit. Professional cycling was a brutal sport, and Paco was certain that if the pressmen who criticised him had to suffer for twelve hours on a bike, over hundreds of kilometres, they might not be so scathing. To truly understand that level of pain and suffering, you had to endure it on a bike and not watch from the comfortable, leather seat of a touring automobile.

Paco probably should have ended his season there, on the road to Colmar, but that was not in his nature. Once he was back in Spain, thoughts of taking a long and comfortable rest in Sopuerta dissolved. He was determined to finish his season on a high but, in the Fifth Grand Prix of Biscay, on the ninth of August, his bad luck returned. He might have considered himself to be the moral victor of the race, which he led for one hundred of the two hundred and fifteen kilometres, but destiny decided otherwise. His tyre burst at the foot of the hill into Morga and a fan, who was talking to him while he was repairing his puncture, told him that his rivals were right behind him. In reality, he had over four minutes advantage on them. Understandably, Paco became nervous and, in his panic, he took much longer to repair the tyre than he normally would; three minutes to be exact. When he finally crested the hill, he looked back and saw Ricardo Montero closing on him. His anxiety increased as he started his descent. Paco was feeling the pressure from his pursuers who were now reeling him in like a fish on a hook. He started taking risks, making decisions he would normally never consider. He fell.

As Paco watched from the gravel road, outstretched, bloodied and bruised, Montero flew past him with a sympathetic glance. So close to the finish, Paco had no way of catching the new leader, but bravely he remounted and continued, arriving at the finish line in third place.

It had been a wretched season compared to the excitement and glory of the previous year. His remarkable debut performance at the Tour de France now seemed like a distant dream and Paco doubted he would ever be able to recapture the form which saw him showered with praise for his courageous ride on

the Galibier. Bicycle racing was proving to be a precarious way
to earn a living. Hours and hours spent in the saddle were no
guarantee of success in the brutal world of international
cycling. It would be two years before Paco returned to the Tour
de France and it would be another heartbreaking experience.

5

CONTROVERSY AND DRAMA: THE 1933 TOUR DE FRANCE

B y the start of the 1932 season, Paco was back on track and his cycling education continued. He was now racing with the Sociedad Ciclista Bilbaín and was nominated for the prestigious cyclists' merit medal. It finally went to Narciso Masferrer Sala and Vicente Trueba, but to be nominated was a great honour. He was also invited to race the Mont Faron climb again. This time, his preparation was meticulous. He had started his winter training early to turn around his fortunes and it proved to be a good tactic. Paco stormed up the climb, finishing in fourth place, ahead of the great French and Tour de France champion, Antonin Mange. Fellow Spaniard, Trueba, could only finish in twelfth place.

The following year, Paco produced another outstanding performance at Mont Faron. It was now a much bigger event but it was a race he knew well. Two hundred riders were invited, and Paco came home in eleventh place. Although he continued to place well in races at home and abroad, it was becoming increasingly clear to him that, at the age of twenty-seven, his winnings would never be enough to wholly support

himself and his family, without the need to find other employ-
ment. He had been physically and emotionally scarred by his
last experience at the Tour de France in 1931 but, by the
summer of 1933, Paco felt a longing to return to it again.

He travelled to Paris with Spain's top rider, Vicente
Trueba, dreaming of rekindling the form he had shown in the
twenty-fourth edition of the race. They were the only two
Spaniards to enter the race and their experiences could not
have been more contrasting. Sadly, the fates conspired against
Paco once again; he was cruelly eliminated after the first stage
in controversial circumstances.

Controversy and drama were synonymous with the Tour
throughout its early history and Henri Desgrange, the auto-
cratic race director, was at the centre of many of the disputes.
It was his inflexibility that led to Paco's elimination from the
Tour in 1933.

On the twenty-seventh of June, on the first stage, from
Paris to Lille, the riders had rolled out of Vésinet in front of
two hundred thousand spectators. Sadly, eight and a half hours
later, when Paco reached the finish at l'hippodrome de Lille, he
had failed to meet the time cut-off by two minutes and thirty
seconds. He was inconsolable. It had been a brutal day. Two
hundred and sixty-two kilometres of frantic racing, including
fifty kilometres over unforgiving cobbles. Paco had suffered
several mechanical problems and punctures and was cut adrift
from the peloton for the majority of the day. As he and Trueba
were now racing as touristes-routiers, they were no longer
eligible for assistance from the mechanical service truck which
they had received in previous years when they had been racing
as Aces for the Spanish National team. Desgrange was not
known for making exceptions to his rulebook, which stated that
any rider finishing more than eight per cent in arrears of the
winner's finishing time would be eliminated from the Tour.
Consequently, Paco was one of nine riders eliminated that day.

However, the decision would come back to haunt Desgrange ten days later.

Paco was back in Sopuerta by the time the riders began the one hundred and fifty-six kilometre, stage ten, from Digne to Nice, on the seventh of July. Desgrange's rule book had ended his dream and he was beginning to believe that, after his incredible debut ride, the stars were somehow now aligned indelibly against him. Sitting at home, he felt like a failure. He had stopped training and his bike was already gathering dust in the outhouse. But when reports of stage ten reached him in Spain, he had every right to feel even more aggrieved at his early elimination from the race.

What should have been a straightforward stage to the Mediterranean was turned on its head when two, unfancied, touristes-routiers, Fernand Fayolle and Fernand Cornez, escaped from the peloton and opened up a significant time gap on the favourites. In Castellane, sixty kilometres from the start, they were fourteen minutes ahead of the main field. In Grasse, their lead had stretched to eighteen minutes and, at the finish, their advantage had extended to twenty-two minutes. Desgrange was now in a very difficult position. If he applied the eight per cent rule, as he had done on stage one when Paco was eliminated, every rider would be eliminated from his race, except the two escapees, plus Pierre Pastorelli, Alfred Bula, Trueba and Léon Le Calvez who, one after the other, had decided to ride away from the disinterested peloton and chase down the leading two riders. Controversially, Desgrange decided to exercise his right to amend his rule book, by increasing the time cut-off limit to ten per cent of the winner's time. His decision meant that all of the favourites were reinstated. Only two riders from the German team, and two individual riders were now eliminated under his new ten per cent rule.

Desgrange's actions stung Paco, but his decision hurt

Trueba even more. Of the first six riders to arrive in Nice that afternoon, Trueba was the leading rider on general classification. After their arrival, the official eight per cent regulatory time limit was quickly reached, which, technically, put Trueba into the yellow jersey. Desgrange had once proudly pronounced that the perfect Tour de France would be one in which only a single rider would survive his race and ride into Paris alone. Had he kept to his rulebook, he might have seen that happen in 1933, and Vicente Trueba could have been the first Spaniard to win the Tour de France. The reality was very different. Desgrange was furious that the two unknowns, Fayolle and Cornez, who, until then, had been anonymous in his race, had put his spectacle in jeopardy. By adjusting his rules, he kept the race alive for the favourites and enabled the French rider, Georges Speicher, to advance up the general standings into third place. Speicher would eventually ride into Paris triumphant, with the yellow jersey on his back. It would be yet another victory for the dominant French team and a major boost to the circulation of Desgrange's newspaper, *L'Auto*. In the last week of the race, sales of his newspaper rose to over eight hundred and fifty thousand copies, a forty-four per cent increase on sales during the 1923 Tour. There was some consolation for Trueba in that he became the first King of the Mountains, a new competition introduced by Desgrange to reward the rider with the best mountain top finishes. Trueba also claimed sixth place in the general classification in Paris, but for Paco there was just a profound emptiness.

Paco's elimination from the Tour continued to gnaw away at him for months afterwards. He could see no future in the sport which he had loved so much and so, reluctantly, he decided to retire from competitions in 1934. He barely looked at his bike and stayed in Sopuerta, at the foot of the incline of Las Muñecas, which had taught him to be a great climber.

Paco had made the most of his travels in Spain and France to educate himself. He was a thoughtful and intelligent young man who was respected in both his town and throughout the region, not solely for his cycling achievements but also for his loyalty, his fairness and his sense of justice. As such, he was nominated to become a Municipal Judge and he was unanimously elected. It was a post which suited his calm and fair-minded character.

His absence from training and competition also meant he had more time to work in his father's grocery store, and the bank of Biscay, which had an agency in the store. He also made regular trips to Bilbao, where his cousin Teresa now lived and worked. He was very fond of her and they would enjoy outings to the theatre or to cafes and restaurants where they would meet with friends. Paco had also started an apprentice-ship course, training to be an electrical engineer. He was beginning to think about the direction his life would take after he had finished his career as a professional cyclist. He occasionally rode his bike in the hills around Sopuerta and to and from Bilbao to see Teresa, but he had no inclination to train or race.

As the following winter approached, it seemed that the end of his professional cycling career would be marked by that controversial exit from the 1933 Tour. Time had gone some way to healing the rawness of that memory, but, secretly, it still haunted him. He was twenty-eight years of age, an age at which most professional cyclists were reaching their peak. He would be twenty-nine by the start of the next Tour de France and it would be the twenty-ninth edition of the race. Surely that was a sign. As a new year beckoned, Paco allowed himself to dream again. Maybe he had one more shot at glory.

He probably should have known better, but cycling had brought him so much joy, excitement and adventure. Realistically, he knew he was unlikely to make the top twenty in the general classification, but to experience the wonderful emotion of finishing in Paris, in front of thousands of ecstatic fans, was surely a realistic goal. Secretly, he still cherished the dream of being the first rider to cross one of the great mountain cols. There would be some great climbers in the 1935 Tour, but Paco had beaten most of them at one time or another in his career, including the red-hot favourite, Antonin Magne, from France.

Paco had plenty to occupy his time and mind at home in Sopuerta, but he missed the thrill of racing. Whenever he worked in the garden and looked up to the hills where he used to train or whenever he turned to acknowledged a group of riders passing his home, memories of his famous ascent of the Galibier in 1930, riding shoulder to shoulder with some of the Tour's greatest riders, came flooding back. They were always accompanied by an aching and a longing. The pull of the Tour was too strong to ignore.

In the year that he had been inactive, the family's modest income had also suffered. Paco made little money from riding the Tour de France, but his racing in Spain, and in the prestigious Mont Faron races, had enabled him to support his family and provide them with some small luxuries, like the motor car he rented for them.

When the bike manufacturer BH, which was based in Eibar, approached Paco to ride for them in the first Vuelta a España, in April 1935, that yearning to race, which had never left him, finally overwhelmed him and he came to the decision to compete again. The first Vuelta would be a massive event for Spain, a landmark occasion, and Paco wanted to be part of it. With ten of the seventeen stages over two hundred and fifty kilometres, it could also provide him with the perfect warm up for a fourth attempt at the Tour de France, in July. A good ride in the Vuelta might earn him a place in the Spanish team of eight for the Tour but, even if he did not make the national team, he was sure he would be good enough to qualify for one of the four individual places set aside for Spanish riders.

If this dream was to become a reality, he would have to start training again with intensity but, first, he faced a difficult conversation with his father. He accepted the offer from BH but had not immediately told his father of his intention, as he knew he would be opposed to his idea of a return to racing. But having committed himself to riding the Vuelta, it was only right that his father should be the first to know.

One morning, father and son were working together in the store.

'Papá, can I speak with you?'

'Of course, Paco. What is it?'

'Well, I have been thinking about this carefully, and I know that you and Mamá will not be happy, but I have decided to make a return to racing.'

His father put down the box of vegetables he was carrying and sighed deeply. 'I have feared this moment Paco. I had a feeling that you have not been entirely happy these last few months, but this makes no sense. You have your responsibilities here now. Your work as a judge and your apprenticeship. Mamá and I thought your cycling was finished with and we were happy that it was.'

'I have had an offer to ride the Vuelta, Papá. The first Vuelta a España and then, if I ride well there, I will have another chance to ride the Tour de France. I will be able to earn more money and help provide for the family again.'

'We would rather have you here, at home, and not risking your life racing. We can manage without the money Paco.'

'It's too late Papá. I have already promised that I will ride in the Vuelta, in April. I intend to resign from my post as Municipal Judge so I can return to full training.'

'This is madness, Paco!' Augustín had raised his voice for the first time.

'I'm sorry Papá but I've made my decision. I miss the life of a professional cyclist and I want to try and finish the Tour one more time. The Tour de France has always been the race of my dreams.'

'Your dream? Your dream? Your dream is a delusion Paco. It has brought you nothing but pain and misery and you must leave it.'

'I cannot Papá,' Paco implored. 'And it's not just the Tour. The first Vuelta a España will be colossal. Can you imagine Papá, an international Vuelta a España?'

'You don't know what you are saying Paco. This cycle racing is too dangerous, too unpredictable. You will die out there on the road. Do you hear me Paco. You will die!' Augustín could feel his voice trembling with emotion.

The father did not want to be saying these things, but this is what he felt, and this is what he feared; that his beautiful son would perish on some godforsaken road, chasing a hopeless dream.

Paco paused for a moment before he spoke again. He had the deepest respect for his father, and, in most situations, he valued his opinions. He was desperate for his father to support his decision to return to racing, but he also sensed that his father would not give way. Augustín had sat down on a stool. His head was bowed in resignation.

'Please listen to me Papá. You are mistaken. I feel as strong as I did in my best years, and I'd be returning with years of experience behind me. Besides, we do need the money that comes from my racing. It pays for the rental and the running of the car and lots of other things.'

Silence followed. It felt like a chasm had opened between father and son. Paco was set on his course and Augustín did not want to argue with his son. He could see that Paco's mind was set in stone and there was nothing more the father could do or say to him to change his mind.

Paco resigned from his work as a judge and, in the weeks that followed, he was increasingly absent from the store. Riding the Vuelta, which would start in Madrid on the twenty-ninth of April, and then returning to Paris in July, for what would probably be his last attempt at the Tour de France, became Paco's only focus.

PART TWO

BACK ON THE BIKE

6

THE FIRST VUELTA A ESPAÑA

P aco began training again with purpose. To begin with, his rides were short and relatively light but his sessions were long and varied, with repetitions of short climbs and sprints. Then he moved on to longer distance rides, to prepare for the stages in the Vuelta which would take over eight hours to complete. The total distance of the race would be three thousand, four hundred and twenty-five kilometres, with the stage to Barcelona being a massive three hundred and ten kilometres. Worryingly, Paco only had a few months to prepare. His brother, Primitivo, joined him on some of his rides but it was not long before Paco became too strong for him. Primitivo was forced to abandon his bike and follow Paco in the family car, offering support and encouragement on the wilder, winter days and providing his brother with a little shelter from the stiff Cantabrian winds.

After a solid winter's training behind him, Paco's comeback came on the thirteen of April, in the Gran Premio de la República. The Trueba brothers, Vicente, Manuel and Fermín rode for the BH team while Paco raced for the Orbea team alongside Salvador Cardona, Mariano Cañardo, Frédérico Esquerra and Eusebio Bastida. The race comprised of four stages from Eibar to Madrid and back. Cardona took the honours and Paco finished nineteenth out of a field of thirty-five. The first stage to Burgos had been a rude awakening for him. He had finished fifth from last, over twenty-six minutes behind the winner of the stage, Cardona. It was what he expected, bearing in mind his time spent in retirement, but the fact he was able to improve his performance as the race progressed did give him confidence ahead of the Vuelta which started two weeks later.

The first Vuelta a España was an ambitious project which had been hastily put together by Juan Pujol, the director of *Informaciones*, the Madrid daily newspaper. As with the Tour de France, organised by *L'Auto* and the Giro d'Italia, run by the *Gazzetta della Sport*, Pujol hoped his race would not only capture the national optimism engendered by the declaration of the new Second Republic, but also lead to an increase in the sales of his newspaper. Attracting some of Europe's biggest cycling stars proved a step too far for the organisers, as most of them were heading to Italy for the Giro which started a few days after the final stage of the Vuelta. However, Pujol had managed to attract eighteen foreign riders who joined the thirty-two Spanish riders. The strongest contingent came from Belgium, who sent six riders. Four came from Italy, and two each travelled from Austria, France, Switzerland and Holland. Paco would be up against some very strong and experienced riders from his own country, as well as some lesser known riders, who were there to make up the numbers. Paco had ridden against many of them and beaten them but he was not yet back to full fitness so he had to be realistic about his chances of success.

Paco knew that, even though they were not the cream of

European talent, the foreign riders would still provide a very stern test. In spite of his growing excitement and cheerfulness, thoughts of winning or even securing a top twenty position had to be set aside. From his home country, his main rivals would be, Salvador Cardona, Mariano Cañardo, Vicente Trueba and Frédérico Ezquerra, his fellow Basque rider. They would carry the home hopes. In some respects this was a relief to Paco. He was making his comeback into the professional ranks, so there would be limited expectations of him. His personal goal was to ride well enough to secure an invitation to the Tour that summer. All the pressure and attention would be on the four leading ranked Spanish riders. Ezquerra had climbed well in the 1934 Tour and, like Paco, in 1930, had won praise from Henri Desgrange after breaking the record for the ascent of the Galibier. Cañardo had finished ninth in the Tour the previous year and Cardona was buoyed from his victory at the GP de la República, a couple of weeks earlier. Vicente Trueba needed no introduction after his previous feats in the Tour de France.

As the international entry was not large enough to divide the riders into national teams, the organisers decided to split the fifty riders into two teams. They would be sponsored by Spain's leading bike manufacturers, BH and Orbea, although it was hard not to believe that, at some point, national alliances would come into play. Paco was assigned to the BH team, along with the Belgians. Although the top Belgians would be riding the Giro or preparing for the Tour, in July, it still looked like they might be the strongest riders in the race. Orbea, which had a fierce rivalry with BH, was not happy.

Orbea had been founded in the nineteenth century and based in the city of Eibar, in the Basque Country. Better known for manufacturing firearms, the company diversified following the First World War and began manufacturing bikes.

BH was founded a little later, in 1909, by three brothers, Domingo, Juan and Cosme Beistegui Albistegui. It also began by producing firearms but, like Orbea, turned to bike manufacturing, starting its operations in 1923.

The start of the race in Madrid was everything Paco expected it to be. Thousands lined the streets of the capital, at seven forty-five in the morning, as the fifty riders set off on their epic, clockwise tour of the country, from outside the Ministry of Works. The mayor dropped his green flag which signalled the start of the neutralised zone. This would take the riders across the capital city in a procession. The crowds were huge, four or five deep along the route, and they applauded and cheered as the riders were led at a fairly sedate pace by motorcyclists from the Civil Guard. Behind the peloton came the usual trail of cars, with officials, radio commentators and the press. Paco was thrilled to be part of this first Vuelta and he could not stop beaming as he and his fellow adventurers ambled across the city. Like the race, his preparations had been hasty, but here he was, participating in a major international tour in his home country.

Mariano Cañardo wore bib number one and Paco was honoured to be given bib number two. The first road stage would take them one hundred and eighty-five kilometres to Vallodolid and, once the peloton reached the Puerta de Hierro, Senor Guiseris signalled the official start and the race was on. Paco was well to the fore and was feeling strong. It would be a hard day's racing. The sky was a brilliant blue and the sun was burning hot, much to the delight of the fans but not so much the riders.

The first man to make a break was the Swiss rider Leo Amberg, who escaped on the climb to León. He rode the twenty-eight kilometres to the summit of the first major climb alone and without having to stop to change his gears. The Spaniards who had their eyes on the prize of one thousand five hundred pesetas, which went to the first rider to arrive at the summit, were closing on the Swiss, but they failed to overhaul him. As is often the case, the riders regrouped on the fast descent and Paco was happy to be in the leading group. They were one hundred kilometres into the stage when the powerful Cañardo went clear with the Belgian, Antonio Digneff. A two metre gap soon turned into two hundred metres, as Spain's number one rider showed his strength and class, towing the Belgian with him. They were motoring along at a steady fifty kilometres per hour. Paco was in a group of sixteen chasers and although the two leaders never built a significant lead, they could not be caught. When Cañardo punctured at a hundred and thirty kilometres, Digneff saw his opportunity and sprinted clear. The Spaniard was able to change his tyre quickly, but he had lost two minutes in that time. He worked hard and managed to catch the Belgian, at one hundred and seventy-two kilometres, and suddenly, at the finish, there was hope for the huge crowd of spectators that there would be a Spanish victory on the opening day. However, their expectations were scuppered when Digneff out-sprinted Cañardo to take the leader's orange jersey. The chase had taken too much out of Cañardo. Paco finished eighteenth, amongst the other favourites, and one of the leading Spanish riders. It had been a great return to big time international racing, but it had also been a very hot and hard stage. The hammer had been put down early.

By the end of stage two, the leader's jersey did end up on the back of a Spaniard. Antonio Escuriet broke away from another dangerous Belgian, Gustaaf Deloor, on the final climb before the finish in Santander and won, to the delight of the ecstatic home fans.

By the third stage, from Bilbao to Santander, it was clear that the Belgians and the Italians were in a class of their own. With the exception of Cañardo, the Spanish riders, including Paco, could not compete, either on the flat or on the climbs.

Paco expected no less after his period of retirement. He was riding not for glory but to reach Madrid. His victory would be to finish the race and in a strong position in the general classification, in relation to the other Spanish riders. Securing an invitation to the Tour de France was always prominent in his mind. It made no sense to risk everything on a crazy breakaway. Better to keep his powder dry.

Paco's task had already been made a little easier on that third morning with the retirement of five Spaniards, David Perez, Manuel Trueba, Antonio Destrieux and Fermín Trueba, the latter with a painful saddle boil. The day began with grey skies and strong headwinds. The poor conditions persisted all the way to San Sebastián and resulted in even more abandonments. Escuriet, had seemed so overwhelmed by his victory on the second day, he had found it difficult to sleep and, following a crash, he was forced to abandon, giving up the leader's jersey to Deloor. Ezquerra, who had exhausted himself from the start of the Vuelta, working for Escuriet, soon joined him and Alvarez, who was hit by a truck, was taken to hospital. Piccardo was the other abandonment and Paco considered himself very fortunate to finish the stage, as the heavens opened. He'd had several mechanical failures and finished in twenty-seventh position, thirty-eight minutes and twenty-three seconds behind the winner, his lowest position yet. He dropped to twenty-first position in the general classification and the reality of professional bike racing hit him squarely in the face. The difficulty of the stage was shown, in that only thirty-six riders remained from the original fifty and at least one of those, Vicente Trueba, looked sick and dejected. It looked doubtful that he would start the next day.

Heavy rain again greeted the riders the following morning as they left San Sebastián, shortly after six o'clock for the long ride to Zaragoza. The lush green hills of the Basque Country would give way to brown plains as the riders sluggishly made inroads into the two hundred and sixty-four kilometres. It was another grim day of wind and rain which only the Belgians and Cañardo seemed to relish. The Belgians could ride all day into driving rain and headwinds and still smile but the Spanish riders craved the sun on their backs. Forty kilometres from Zaragoza, Vicente Trueba retired. On arriving at Zaragoza, there was another appreciative crowd waiting. Such was their enthusiasm they crowded into the road, forcing the riders to ride in single file through a tunnel of applause. They crossed the city, dodging spectators, cars and trams, at speeds of forty-five kilometres per hour, until they finally reached the Torrero velodrome, where the race exploded into a fierce sprint. Cañardo won, restoring some Spanish pride.

Stage Six took the riders to Barcelona on another long and miserably wet and windy stage. The riders started at seven-thirty in the morning in their rubber raincoats. The stage was painfully slow for most of the day, which suited Paco after his time losses. Fifty kilometres from Barcelona, with a timid and watery sun emanating from the Mediterranean, the race was ignited by François Adam, and Max Bulla. These two crushed the peloton with their power and they sprinted away to contest the stage. Paco rallied well and finished in the top ten, only seven minutes down on Adam and seven seconds behind Cañardo, the best of the Spaniards. His doggedness won him praise from the *ABC* race reporters, who marvelled at his performance. 'Always modest, always cheerful, he rides as a hobby, for the love of the bike and for a sense of adventure. He is the complete cyclist.' Paco enjoyed reading the race reports when they were complimentary, but the Vuelta had been harder than he had expected, and he welcomed the first rest day in Barcelona more.

After the rest day, the stage to Valencia would be flat and pose few problems for the leading Belgians who were used to this terrain. The weather, which continued to be unseasonably poor, was also in their favour. In spite of the rain, the crowds again came out in force but under the cover of their umbrellas. On the rest day, the journalists had been pressing the Spanish riders for an explanation for their relatively poor performances. Paco was one of the few Spanish riders to have impressed. He was having a magnificent Vuelta considering he had been out of the sport. He also pointed to his bad luck in the early stages with mechanical failures. With better fortune, he might have been amongst the leaders, but as many professional riders will agree, how often is this the case?

'I haven't been able to recover the time I have lost,' Paco lamented. 'In addition, on the flat stages, the Belgians rest and fuel themselves. The foreign riders are riding together, and they are better suited to the rain and the mud than the Spanish. We love the sun. The heat and the poor road surfaces of Andalusia are coming and this should suit the home riders. We will try our best but there will be no battle if the foreigners don't try.'

Paco was right. There was no battle. The stage to Valencia started in thick fog and the pace was pedestrian, not that the crowds seemed to mind. They applauded much the same as they would if the riders had been racing flat out. It made the 'heroes of the road' feel a little guilty as they rode more like tourers than racers. Barely one hundred kilometres were covered in four hours. The race had already seen many abandonments but there was no danger of that number being added to on a day such as this. At twenty kilometres per hour, the peloton meandered along roads boarded by cypress and orange trees. The skies remained grey and the rain started to fall again. The funeral pace seemed to be in keeping with the gloomy skies and the uncharacteristically murky Mediterranean. The peloton's mood was only slightly lifted by workers who handed the riders oranges from the roadside. The pace picked up a little at Villarreal and there were a few skirmishes. The Belgians, splattered with mud, tried to escape and the peloton lengthened, but then everything came back together. As Valencia came into view, the sun finally emerged from behind the clouds and the riders were able to remove their raincoats, but it was not until the final five hundred metres that Bulla and the Dutchman, Gerrit Van der Ruit, went full throttle to the line, with the Austrian taking the win. Deloor stayed in orange and Paco settled for fifth place, twenty-two seconds behind the winner.

For stage nine, the riders rose at three in the morning and were on the road by four. The route took the riders two hundred and sixty-five kilometres from Valencia to Murcia. The roads were once again veiled in mist and men from the north, like Paco, who were used to the humidity, began to curse the rain and mud. The torrents fell from the leaden skies. It was in their bones. This would be another day of purgatory for the riders as the roads became rivers of mud under the storm. On arriving at the food tables, the men became an unruly mob, helping themselves to bowls of dynomogen. They asked for coffee, hot water, and cognac, to warm and revitalise their exhausted bodies. On the descent into Benidorm, Paco and Cañardo tried to escape but the Belgians shut them down. After the control at Benisa, they planned to try again but the attack never came.

The descents were death traps, and, near Campello, the road was covered in a thick layer of clay which sent the following cars sliding and careering from one ditch to the other. A curve suddenly swallowed up a group of riders and their bikes. They were sprawled on the ground, groaning and moaning and plastered with mud. Gonzalez was in extreme pain, with a deep wound to his knee. Another rider had dislocated his arm and another had terrible grazes to his thigh. The doctor was kept busy tending to the injured. It looked like a battlefield. The Asturian, Agustín González, could not continue but the Italian, Paolo Bianchi, insisted that he could ride on after lengthy treatment.

The peloton pressed on regardless and Bianchi did not return to the fold for over two hours, covered in bloodied bandages. The Spaniards had been planning to take the fight to the Belgians, who had a strangle hold on the race, but they had not bargained on this unrelenting battle with the elements.

The sun did briefly show its face in Alicante but only the enthusiasm of the vast crowds warmed the hearts of the riders. However, chaos awaited them in the busy town of Moteagudo, dominated by its red castle and the impressive Christ figure which stood above it. It was market day and the riders had to weave their way between the crowds. The finish in Murcia was only four kilometres away and there was the usual acceleration for the line where, again, some pride was restored with Cardona and Cañardo disputing the sprint. Paco was only six seconds adrift. He was given third place on the stage and was happy with his position of eighteenth in the general classification out of the thirty-one riders still left in the race.

The hope that the dusty roads of Andalusia would offer more opportunities for Paco and the Spaniards failed to materialise. The sun shone, eventually, which was a welcome relief from the mud and the rain that had, for days, sapped the will and the resolve of the riders to race. Their spirits deadened, they seemed resigned to a Belgian victory and so they meandered their way northwards from Seville. To most of the riders, it felt that riding into Madrid would be victory enough. Most were suffering from stomach problems and fatigue from nights of fragmented sleep. Only the Belgians seemed unscathed. They looked as fresh as they had done at the start line in Madrid. Their lives seemed charmed.

Paco and Fernand Fayolle, from France, did their best to stretch the peloton whenever the road climbed, but neither possessed the power to force a break away. They simply towed the field to the cols and merely offered a springboard to others who claimed the mountain points. By the twelfth stage Paco had won a measly two points in the mountains' competition.

By the penultimate stage from Cáceres to Zamora, it seemed that the major interest would be whether or not Francisco Mula could hold onto his last position and claim the coveted lantern rouge and a prize of one hundred pesetas. He had gone to extraordinary lengths to secure the final position in the general classification, and he was determined not to lose his prize in the final days. He trusted no one and watched the peloton like a hawk, constantly counting the remaining twenty-nine riders in case one of his rivals drifted to the back. They might be hiding in a bush until the peloton had disappeared up the road, and then emerge with a considerable time deficit. Mula knew all the tricks. As soon as he saw a rider become detached, he would slow down and ride alongside them. He would then slowly drag them back to the head of the peloton, where he would deposit them, before taking up his position at the back once again. He enjoyed the attention associated with being the last placed rider; the interviews, the cheers and the applause he received from the roadside.

'Let's see how it turns out,' said the man from Madrid. Everyone knows that I am the last one on the road. I've honestly earned those hundred pesetas and made too many sacrifices to have my prize taken away from me before we arrive in Madrid. Only then will I happily throw myself into a ditch.'

Earning the prize for finishing last was no straightforward matter. Nothing is easy or comfortable at the Vuelta a España.

Mula's antics were only a humorous sideshow in what proved to be the most spectacular stage of the Tour. The riders departed fifteen minutes late, at a quarter to six in the morning; delays were now becoming a feature of the race. It was a bright and sunny morning which meant that, later in the day, hands and arms would be burning on the bars. Twenty-nine kilometres in and Cañardo had his first mechanical problem. He was determined to protect his second position overall, knowing that victory was beyond his reach, as the Belgians and many of the foreign riders were now working together for Deloor. Bianchi was an exception. The Italian had worked tirelessly and faithfully for Cañardo and, once again, helped pace him back to the main group. A puncture or mechanical at any time in a stage is frustrating and demoralising for the rider but, if they are to occur, better to have a problem at the beginning of the day rather than in the final twenty kilometres. This day would be dominated by kilometres and kilometres of sky and plains of dust and hellish roads. There would be numerous punctures and Amberg would break his front forks. Mula was in for a busy day, patrolling the back of the bunch.

After one hundred and twenty-seven kilometres, the Belgians made a move to isolate Cañardo. Not content with the overall victory for Deloor, they now wanted to deprive Cañardo of his second place. After an attack from Isidro Figueras and Bianchi, to contest a sprint, had been brought back by the peloton, Digneff attacked on a climb. The Deloor brothers and the other Belgians blocked Cañardo but Paco saw what was afoot and went to the front, towing Edoardo Molinar, Amberg, Luigi Barral, Fayolle, Salvador Molina and Cañardo, the latter being carefully marshalled by Gustav Deloor, to the top. There Digneff's lead had quickly grown to a minute, despite the efforts of Paco to bring him back. The foreign riders were aligning with the Belgians and the Spaniards were doing their best to protect Cañardo's second place on the podium. The descent towards Béjar was fast, with Digneff maintaining his minute's advantage. If anything, it had slightly grown. Although Cañardo had started the day with a minute and thirty-two seconds advantage over Digneff, his second place overall was looking exceedingly fragile. The Belgians had grouped themselves at the head of the peloton so that they could block the efforts of the pursuers. At the worst possible time, fate intervened again in the life of Paco. He punctured and soon became a solitary figure, on this dusty stretch of road, as the peloton ploughed on. The bicycle is the perfect machine when it works, the rider's best friend, but when it fails, when the chain breaks, for example, or a tyre bursts, all the effort of thousands of kilometres, all the sweat deployed for hours and hours, all the hunger and thirst that has been suffered and all the sun that has been burning bare skin, is completely useless.

Moments later Barral, the leader of the mountains' competition 'hit the wall'. He climbed off his bike and signalled to the first car that approached him that he was finished. His tank was empty. He had nothing more to give and the chasing group was another man down.

That morning, Cañardo had probably lost hope of eating into the eight-minute deficit to the race leader Deloor, and the rest of the Spanish riders, Paco included, were longing for the finish in Madrid. The four o'clock wake up calls for breakfast were beginning to take their toll. The Belgians plan to isolate Cañardo had briefly galvanised the Spaniards into action and given them a reason to ride, but the pursuit was losing strength and Digneff was now extending his overall lead over Cañardo.

Sixty kilometres from Salamanca, the riders were racing across a dry, rocky and dusty landscape. Digneff now had a three-minute lead. In the next instant, Deloor attacked the peloton and set off in search of his teammate Digneff. It was an extraordinary move which took the main chasing group by surprise. Deloor had no need to extend his lead further. Perhaps his plan was to join Digneff, to help him in his escape, or perhaps he too was worried about his teammate going for the overall victory himself; after all, Deloor had less than ten minutes advantage over Digneff.

Cañardo, back in the peloton, could do nothing, but he still had the support of his faithful domestique, Bianchi, and his fellow Spaniards Américo Tuero, Cardinal, Esteve, Fayolle, and Paco, who had defied all the odds by making it back to the main peloton following his puncture. This was no mean feat, as Cañardo's group was charging along at fifty kilometres an hour in the pursuit of the two Belgians.

Deloor was never able to make contact with his teammate, Digneff, before he was brought back to the main group with Paco's help. One fire had been extinguished but Digneff was still the main danger to Cañardo. With fifty kilometres remaining in the stage, Paco's group finally caught a tiring Digneff and peace was at last restored. It seemed that the calm would last until the final kilometre when there would be the usual sprint for the line but anyone who follows professional cycling will know that nothing is certain and a race can be blown apart in a moment with an attack or a mechanical or God forbid an accident.

Then it happened. Eleven kilometres from the finish, Cañardo cruelly fell victim to such a moment, enabling the leading riders to go clear again. Bianchi remained with him but it was unclear whether his other allies, Paco included, knew about his misfortune because they pressed on regardless.

In the sprint in Zamora, the Italian, Molinar, won, and led home a group that included the Deloor brothers, Digneff and Paco, who finished a creditable thirteen. He had moved up the standings one place, with Barral's abandonment, and was now in seventeenth position. But Cañardo's nightmare continued. The crowds watched anxiously, waiting for their hero to arrive. Two minutes passed and Bianchi came into view, but Cañardo was not with him. It looked like he had done all he could to help the Spaniard but had finally accepted defeat in trying to bring the Cañardo back to the front of the race. It was almost another three minutes before Cañardo finished. A disaster. He had tumbled from second overall to fourth and was now three minutes and forty-seven seconds behind Digneff. The Belgian had firmly supplanted him in second position in the overall standings.

On the final morning, the riders shrugged off their aches and pains and their weariness and left Zamora, at twenty to eight, and began the last two hundred and fifty kilometres into a stiff and bitter headwind. It was not raining but the riders wore their waterproofs to protect themselves from the wind chill. The wind blew stronger and stronger and the riders felt that they were making no progress. In the first hour, they barely covered twenty-four kilometres and they were cold to the bone. Add to that the terrible condition of the road. Paco was already looking forward to his hot shower and a good meal but that would be several hours away.

Finally, some respite came. After Tordesillas, the road improved and the peloton had the benefit of a tail wind. It was a relief for the riders but not for Américo Tuero, who quite suddenly fell heavily. The young rider, from Madrid, had been dreaming about the finish in his home city since the start of the race but now that dream was in shreds.

He got to his feet and screamed, 'I'm finished. I can't go on.'

The doctors rushed to him and patched him up and, covered in bandages, he rejoined the race. When the rider has the will, the impossible becomes possible.

As the riders headed towards the finish line, music and fireworks, in the towns and villages through which they passed, added to the spectacle and excitement. The crowds had been one of the outstanding features of the race. They had done Spain proud. With the Guadaramma mountain range ahead in the mist, it started to drizzle but the race was about to liven up and Paco was at the front of the train. He drove the group up the main climb with the intention of weakening the resolve of Digneff and Molina, the two men now ahead of Cañardo, after his unlucky time loss the previous day. Paco was forced to give way at the summit to Molinar, who took the points and the prize money, but he was still well placed and, more importantly, his efforts had stretched out the field. Surprisingly, for the first time, the Belgians had been sleeping and they were slightly distanced. This was the opportunity Cañardo had been waiting for. He attacked on the descent into Guadaramma and he took Bulla with him. They threw caution to the wind, reaching terrifying speeds of eighty kilometres per hour. By the time they entered the town, the pair had been joined by Deloor but there was no sign of Digneff and Molinar.

Cañardo saw his opportunity to right the wrong of the previous day and continued to apply the pressure. Fortunately, as Bulla also had his eyes on a podium position, as he had started the day in fifth place in the overall standings, he was happy to ride with the Spaniard. The pair alternated at the front reaching speeds of more than sixty kilometres per hour. Deloor, of course, did nothing but suck on the wheels of the two men in front. They were less than forty kilometres from the finish in Madrid where a huge crowd was waiting for them. The Belgians in the group behind tried to bring the peloton back to the leading three, but their efforts were futile, as both Cañardo and Bulla were riding like their lives depended on it.

As Cañardo, Bulla and Deloor, entered the streets of Madrid and headed for the finish line, in the Avenue of the Chestnuts, it was clear that the stage would come down to a sprint finish between the three of them. In the end, it was Deloor, who had been conserving his energy, by riding on the wheels of the other two who won, to put added shine on his overall victory. Cañardo snatched second, with Bulla third.

Next, there was the agonising wait for the rest of the field and, in particular, Digneff and Molinar. The clock kept ticking and to everyone's relief four minutes passed with no rider in view. In fact, it was almost ten minutes before the next rider,

Amberg, appeared. Seconds later, the group containing Digneff arrived. He must have known he had lost his second place to Cañardo because he did not even contest the sprint. Paco, however, did. He wanted to end his Vuelta on a high and was narrowly squeezed into sixth place by Vicente Bachero. It had been a great day for Spain and Paco was especially proud of the crucial role he had played in Cañardo's triumph. He had worked selflessly all day and his strong performance would hopefully not go unnoticed by the organisers of the Tour de France.

It had been a remarkable day and an even more remarkable comeback for Cañardo. He had turned a four-minute deficit to Digneff into a seven-minute advantage. Cañardo had not won the First Vuelta a España, but he had certainly won the hearts of the Spanish fans for his boldness and tenacity. Sadly for Bulla, his mammoth effort with Cañardo was not enough to overhaul Digneff but, as Molinar finished fifteen minutes down, he was able to leapfrog him into fourth place.

It had been an unexpected and exciting finish to the race which had suffered its ups and downs. Unquestionably, every rider who had finished this gruelling race deserved praise.

The three thousand, one hundred and seventy-five kilometres had been ridden at an average speed of twenty-eight and half kilometres per hour. Paco knew that the Tour de France would be much faster and the mountain climbs more severe, but he was happy with his seventeenth position. Of the thirty-two Spanish riders who had started the race, Paco had been beaten by only four, Cañardo, Cardona, Juan Gimeno and Bâchero. He was immensely proud that he had not only ridden his country's first Tour but he had completed it in the face of some terrible weather conditions and on very poor road surfaces. He now believed he could go on and tackle the Tour de France in two months, but he would need to train hard, as soon his body had recovered from the Vuelta. The average speeds in the Tour de France would be thirty-six kilometres per hour on the flat stages and up to thirty kilometres per hour in the mountains. It would be an even bigger test for Paco but he felt a surge of confidence from his ride. The big question was, would he be given an invitation to the Tour on the strength of his Vuelta ride?

7

RETURN TO PARIS

A ny lingering doubts about whether Paco would be riding in the twenty-ninth Tour de France were swept away when Henri Desgrange sent out his recruiters. Gaston Bénac, a sports journalist with *Paris Soir*, who had previously worked for Desgrange at *L'Auto*, was instructed to call on Paco and invite him to race as a Spanish individual. As soon as the telegram arrived, informing Paco that Bénac was on his way, he could hardly contain his excitement. On his training rides, he suddenly felt more alive and he rode harder and longer and when Bénac finally arrived in Sopuerta, four weeks before the start of the Tour de France, Paco signed the contract without hesitation. The twenty-ninth Tour de France in his twenty-ninth year. He would have one final shot at the most famous bike race in the world.

Paris, 1st July 1935

It was a beautiful summer's day when Paco's train arrived at Quai d'Orsay. The Tour would start in three days and it was one of Monsieur Desgrange's many rules that all the riders had to be in Paris no later than three days before the event. It was also a tradition that every Tour rider should visit *L'Auto's* editorial office.

Paco first checked into the Hôtel Bohy-Lafayette, on rue La Fayette, where he showered and changed his clothes. He then headed to the newspaper's offices at ten rue du Faubourg-Montmartre. It was a ten-minute walk and Paco took his time. He loved the excitement of being in Paris. He could stroll amongst the crowds, while others hurried along in their smart suits and hats, striding out as if they had somewhere important to be. The cafes were full and customers spilled out onto the pavements where they enjoyed a coffee and a cigarette under the shade of an awning. Some were engrossed in newspapers whilst others were locked in animated conversations. A few lolled back in their chairs, enjoying a brief respite from the busyness and the bustle of city life. Paco was now a world away from the rural tranquility of his Basque town. His next adventure had truly started and he wanted to soak up the atmosphere, thinking this would probably be his final Tour de France.

When the familiar *L'Auto* sign came into view, Paco saw a crowd of people, mainly men and small boys, huddled outside the front door. They had gathered in the hope of catching sight of one of the favourites and to collect some autographs. To his surprise, he was recognised and immediately surrounded. Paco loved the thrill that the race generated in the citizens of the capital. He was always happy to talk with fans, even though his French was very simple. Many of the riders were dour and serious and disliked this duty, seeing it as yet another decree imposed upon them by the formidable Monsieur Desgrange. Paco was not like that. For the most part, he loved the attention from the journalists, the photographers, and the small, eager boys, who pushed their way to the front of the crowd, in the hope that they might sneak into a picture which could appear in one of the many daily newspapers. Paco took it all in his stride. He was happy to play his part in the great show. He was particularly at ease with the children. In past Tours, at the beginning of every stage, he would often be found with a gaggle of enthusiastic kids dragging at his heels. With younger brothers and a younger sister, Paco knew how to amuse the little ones. They would clutch pen pictures of the riders and they would try to pick them out and ask them for autographs. Some would just stand, open mouthed, in awe, while others were eager to shake the hand of one of their heroes or simply run their small hands over the cold steel of the riders' bikes.

Once in the newspaper offices of *L'Auto*, everybody was very friendly, and Paco received quite a lot of attention, especially from the office girls. He was a handsome young man with his dark hair greased and swept back, as was the fashion. In spite of his small stature, Paco stood out in a crowd, with his tanned skin and his dark, intense eyes. His complexion had earned him the nickname 'el negro' in the peloton. He could not exactly remember how he came by the name, but most of the riders had nicknames and Paco accepted his.

On his trip to *L'Auto's* offices, Paco wore his best striped jacket, a striped shirt, and a very debonair, red bow tie with white spots. Two of the world's greatest sprinters, Charles Pélissier and Raffaele Di Paco, always wore well-cut suits and favoured the bow tie and Paco enjoyed following the latest fashion. He prided himself on his appearance and, without doubt, looked quite the gentleman. Two of the office girls asked him for an autograph and he happily obliged. He shook numerous hands and did his best to answer a few questions, in his rudimentary French. Sensibly, he had prepared a few sentences.

'I am very happy to be here in Paris.' 'I hope to ride a good race.' 'I would like to thank Monsieur Desgrange for inviting me to this year's Tour de France.'

He found speaking in French quite a strain but considered

it his duty to fulfil the obligations outlined in his contract; it was not in his nature to be grumpy about it like some of the other riders, notably the Aces. The Aces were the elite professional riders who were sponsored by one of the leading bicycle manufacturers or who had been selected to ride as one of a team of eight by their National Federations. Paco had been an Ace in the past, but, in the 1935 Tour, he had been invited to ride as an individual. Whatever his status, Paco was by nature a joyful character who was happy to carry out his duties. He barely knew another way. Nevertheless, he was also fastidious about his race preparation and he was anxious not to spend too much time on his legs before the start of the race. He had already had a long and tiring train journey and he still had some important preparations that needed attending to. When it was time to leave, he took a complimentary copy of *L'Auto* which had published a list of the riders who were competing in the race. The riders were grouped in their national teams but, as Paco was riding as an individual, he had to scan down to that section before he could find his name. He could not help but smile when he read his own profile.

'Francisco **CEPEDA**: The Spanish rider has already ridden a good race in the Tour de France when he was particularly courageous. He is not a classy rider but he is a rider who is always in the running. It could well be that in a test like the Tour de France, where tenacity is needed, he is one of the best riders that Spain has and he climbs well too. But he could be too easily isolated. He is another short rider. However, along with Trueba, he is a true athlete. He is brown, tanned and clever like a monkey and he is providence to the journalist, always having a funny story at his fingertips. There are no limits to his talents. He is a specialist in the mountains and a master in the art of climbing.'

By the time he arrived back at the hotel it was late. Late for everybody else he thought. As he had not changed the time on his watch, he was still operating on Spanish time, so it felt early for him. Hôtel Bohy-Lafayette specialised in hosting sports teams and it was Henri Desgrange's choice for all the riders, including the Aces and the officials. Furnished in the American style, it had two restaurants, numerous lounges, an American bar and four elevators. In the past, Paco had always shared a room with another rider, usually someone from the Spanish team, but on this occasion he had his own room. It was very small but comfortable. He had a small single bed, a writing table and chair and a narrow wardrobe. There was one bathroom at the end of the hallway which several riders shared.

Hotel Bohy was where the riders would congregate in the days before the Grand Départ and this is where they would return, for a well-earned rest, in a month, after their hard struggles on the roads of France. It was probably the best hotel the riders would use during the the Tour. The French Aces were usually roomed on the ground floor of the hotels, whereas the foreign riders, especially the climbing specialists, were usually given rooms on the top floor. There was nothing worse for a rider, at the end of a tortuous ten-hour mountain stage than having to scale seven flights of stairs to get to his bed.

Paco headed directly to the hotel restaurant, as his stomach was beginning to grumble. All the Aces of the Tour were divided into their National teams. They sat at long tables and each table had a small flag, indicating each team's nation. Paco walked past the Spanish team table and shook hands with his friends, before finding his place on the tables designated for the independents.

He was reminded of a funny incident that had happened when he rode his second Tour, in 1931, as the sole Spanish rider. On that occasion, when he arrived for supper, the room had again been full, except for the Spanish team table which was set for eight but, naturally, was empty. He sat down at the table and ordered his meal. Paco's French may have been basic but when it came to eating, he made every effort to be understood.

'Garçon!' cried Paco. He indicated to the waiter that he was ready to eat, by miming the action of eating with his hands. He dare not attempt too much French for fear of appearing foolish.

'I am sorry, sir,' the waiter replied. 'I was told to wait until you are complete.' The waiter smiled at Paco and left.

Paco was mystified by the waiter's response but he naturally assumed that the waiter had left to promptly produce a meal. By this point he was starving and beginning to feel a little light-headed.

After ten, fifteen and then thirty minutes without seeing even a soup bowl appear, Paco's stomach was feeling cavernous, so he asked again.

'The maître d'hotel, please? I've been waiting for half an hour.'

'Pas possible.'

'How is it not possible?'

'We need to wait for your seven colleagues to arrive. Only when the team is complete can the meal be served.'

Finally, Paco saw an end to the confusion.

'But I am the only member of the team,' explained Paco. 'I am a team of one. Now the meal! Where is the meal?'

'You are the only one?'

The waiter had also finally realised his mistake. He made his apologies and, in an instant, returned with Paco's supper, much to the relief of his aching stomach.

Now, facing what would probably be his final Tour, only days away, eating his supper, as an individual rider, Paco felt a similar feeling of isolation. The Spanish team was sitting at the other end of the dining room, with the other National teams and, although Paco would have the opportunity to talk and relax with the Spanish riders between the stages, he would not be riding with them or for them. He would have to make alliances with other individuals or touristes-routiers, as he had done in 1931. This would be essential in order to survive the Tour and make it to Paris, which remained his primary goal, along with his dream of leading the race over a historic col.

Following supper, Paco exchanged a few words with friends from former years, before retiring to his bed. It had been a long and tiring day and he still had to collect his bike which he would do the next day, after breakfast.

The following morning, he headed off to the Vélodrome d'Hiver, which was situated on corner of the boulevard de Grenelle and rue Néalton, close to the famous Eiffel Tower. Paco had a spring in his step, as the Vélodrome was where the special yellow bikes, on which they would ride the Tour de France, were stored. Desgrange had opened the indoor velodrome in 1909, the first of its kind in France. It hosted six-day races and drew vast crowds. Paco glanced inside the stadium before heading downstairs to where the bikes were stored. It was an imposing track. The cliff-like banking was frightening. Paco had experience of track racing but not on a track as steep as this. It was hard to imagine how the riders could stay upright. Above the track, there were also two tiers of steep seating which could accommodate twenty thousand spectators.

The rich and famous would be trackside, close to the action, and Ernest Hemingway was a frequent visitor during his time in Paris.

Paco's thoughts soon returned to his bike. This was always an exciting but anxious moment. The riders had to send their bike measurements to the race organisers, with the length of the cranks required, before the twenty-fifth of May so they could be built in time for the race. However, until he actually saw the bike Paco was always nervous. How would the bike look? Would it be the right size? He was eager to see it, touch it, to put his own mark upon it, to adjust the seat and adapt the machine to his own measurements and preferences.

The bikes, in their gleaming yellow livery were standing in racks and, after he had identified himself to the mechanics, Paco was taken to the machine bearing the number sixty. This was the number that he had be given in this year's race. He could barely contain his excitement. He wheeled the bike to a remote corner of the building, leaned it carefully against the wall, and stood back and admired it.

'What a beauty you are,' he murmured to himself, running his fingers across the smooth steel of the top tube. He then tried the handle bars for size. Perfect. The paintwork on the bike was immaculate, unlike the bike he rode at home which was covered with chips and scuffs. The brakes, the tin bottles, sealed with corks and held in a metal cage on the handlebars, and the duralumin wheels, one of Henri Desgrange's innovations for this year's race, gleamed in their newness. Paco felt an intimacy with his bikes and for the next three weeks this machine would be his friend and hold his confidences.

But as good as it looked, he needed to make it ready. Mechanics were available to the riders but Paco wanted to prepare the machine himself. He put on some blue overalls and began to set everything in order. Nothing better than the master's eye. He adjusted the height of the saddle and the handlebars and fine-tuned the brakes. Finally, he turned his attention to the controversial new duralumin wheels, making sure the tubular tyres sat perfectly on the metal rims. The rims were the latest technology, replacing the tried and trusted wooden rims to which the riders had been accustomed. Desgrange had accepted an offer, and a considerable sum of money, from a German firm who were keen to supply the riders with their new, lighter, more rigid wheels. In the past, Desgrange had been sceptical about metal rims, fearing that the tyres would not adhere to them. He thought the advantage the rider would gain in weight was minimal so, as he did with most new technology that had been offered to him by the bicycle manufactures, like the introduction of derailleur gears, he had rejected it. Desgrange had already sidelined and angered the leading bike manufacturers with his introduction of national teams but, in doing so, he now had many more expenses to pay than in the days when the riders were sponsored by the bike companies. One way of recouping some of the money he was having to pay out to support the riders, who otherwise would have been sponsored by brands like Peugeot, Automoto or Alcyon, was to allow companies, of his choosing, to pay for the privilege of showcasing their goods. Hence the introduction of the metal rims for the first time. Paco had never ridden on metal rims before and was unsure about how they would feel when he rode the bike. He was not entirely happy that his first experience of riding on the new wheels would come on stage one of world's toughest race, but it was something to which he and the other riders would have to adapt. Paco was meticulous when it came to checking and preparing his bike and he planned to spend most of the morning in the workshop.

As he worked away intently, a muscular group of blond, young men startled him. They looked far from friendly as they approached him and they gestured for him to go with them.

Curious and feeling a little intimidated, Paco followed them to a group of Tour bicycles. They seemed to want him to do something. Paco tried talking to them in French but got blank, intense stares in return.

'What is it?' he asked. 'What do you want?'

'We are Germans!' they replied, looking rather aggressive.

Paco now thought he understood. 'So you are riders from the German team? I am also a rider and therefore your friend but, right now, I need to finish preparing my bike.'

Paco turned his back on the bemused looking Germans and headed back to his bike on the other side of the workshop. One of them followed him and violently grabbed hold of the collar of his overalls and dragged him back. Paco was thrust against the wall. His heart leapt and he let out a splutter.

'What is it? What do you want?'

Luckily for him, at that very moment, one of *L'Auto's* mechanics arrived on the scene. Paco recognised him as a friend and, fortunately, he recognised Paco. Mercifully, he could also speak some German. The Germans had thought Paco was a mechanic. The misunderstanding was soon cleared up but that did not completely excuse their behaviour.

When Paco had been released from the vice-like grip of the largest of the Germans, he straightened his overalls and attempted one of his signature smiles.

'My friends, I am a rider like you!'

Suddenly the atmosphere changed and there was laughter all around.

When Paco returned to the hotel, his race package was waiting for him. He took it immediately to his hotel room. Paco remembered that before the 1931 Tour, he had opened the package to find a red and yellow race jersey. This had come as a shock to him, as they were the old Spanish colours. Since the downfall of General Miguel Primo de Rivera's government in 1930 and the exile of King Alfonso XIII, Spain had gone through a period of political upheaval, where coalitions of socialist parties competed with conservative factions for political control. With the declaration of the Second Republic, the Interim Government had enacted a decree, on 27th April 1931, requiring the adoption of a tricolour national flag, comprising of three horizontal strips of equal width; the upper being red, the central being yellow and the lower dark purple. It replaced the red and yellow flag which was associated with the deposed Bourbon monarchy. Paco assumed that the French had not heard of the change in colours since the declaration of the Second Republic, but he did not feel it was his place to correct Monsieur Desgrange. Who was he? - Francisco Cepeda, a relatively unknown rider, hired to ride the Tour de France. Nevertheless, as Paco was the sort of person who liked to be correct, it did play on his mind. However, it was not until moments before the start of the first stage that he finally plucked up the courage to alert Monsieur Desgrange to the potential problem.

'Monsieur Desgrange, I have been given a jersey in the same Spanish colours that the Spanish team wore last year.'

'What's the problem? Are you afraid of wearing this jersey?' replied Desgrange.

'I do not have a different one. So, I am wearing the one that I have been given.'

'But will anything happen to you if you are seen wearing it?' asked Monsieur Desgrange.

'No, I don't think so. Besides I will take responsibility,' replied Paco confidently.

'If there are shots, it will be your problem,' Desgrange asserted.

'I do not think there will be a problem. In Spain, they know me.'

'Well, just in case, when we arrive in Bayonne, we will give you a jersey with the current colours.'

'When you order me to do so, I will take this one off and I will put on the other one. After all, I cannot ride without a jersey.' Paco laughed.

There was no confusion on this occasion. Paco would have loved to have worn his national colours. Riding for Spain was a great honour and one which he cherished, but he realised that, having been out of the sport for most of the previous season, he had lost his ranking in the Spanish racing scene. He was here as an individual rider and a guest of the Tour de France and so he would wear individual colours. He laid out his jersey on his bed. He may not be representing Spain but he still looked with pride at his grey jersey with the purple stripe, which was a sign of his Spanish blood.

Later that afternoon, as Paco was relaxing in the hotel lounge, a smartly dressed young man from the hotel staff approached him with an envelope.

'This letter just arrived for you, Monsieur Cepeda.'

Paco looked surprised but thanked him and took the letter. He did not recognise the handwriting, so he opened it eagerly to reveal its contents. What he saw next rendered him speechless.

'His majesty, the Infante, Don Juan, Prince of Asturias, has requested me to invite you to meet with him at Hotel Meurice, tomorrow afternoon at 3pm. He requests that you bring your bicycle with you, if possible.'

The letter was signed by The Viscount of Rocomora, the Infante's secretary.

Paco had to pinch himself. He could not quite believe it. He had heard that the Prince might be in Paris but why would he wish to meet a humble young man from a small Basque town? In March, the Prince, the heir apparent to the Spanish throne, had completed his training with the British Navy, at

Dartmouth, but now he had returned to Paris where his father, King Alonso XIII, had sought refuge, following his exile from Spain in April 1931.

It had been a torrid time for the Spanish Royal family. A few years before the family's enforced exile, the Spanish public had thronged the streets around the royal palace in a show of support for the monarchy but, in 1931, they chanted death threats to the King and Queen, as a Second Republic was formed in a peaceful revolution. Juan, the third son of the King, was sailing towards Gibraltar at the time, in his training as a midshipman. Fearing for his life Juan, dressed in civilian clothes, had headed first to Rome, before later joining his father in Paris. The King had escaped from the Royal Palace, in Madrid, the night before the Second Republic was formally announced. If he had stayed, he would almost certainly have been arrested and tried for treason, possibly facing the death penalty. As it was, he arrived in Paris, by train, and was given a hero's welcome at the station by a huge crowd made up of sympathetic French supporters and Spanish exiles. The queen and their children joined the King the following day.

Since the beginning of the century, the Spanish Royal family had been regular visitors to French capital. When in Paris, their home was Le Meurice, one of the city's most resplendent hotels. The king rented Suites 106 to 108 and even brought his own furniture with him. The King of Montenegro, the Prince of Wales, King George VI, French President Doumergue, the Sultan of Zanzibar, the Maharaja of Jaïpur, and the Grand Duchess of Russia were all regular guests of the hotel and so it became known as the Hôtel des Rois, the Hotel of Kings. Once exiled, the Spanish Royal family naturally returned to Le Meurice, before, later, renting a private wing of the Savoy Hotel in Fointainebleu. Life in Paris was good, until the Spanish authorities finally applied enough pressure on the French Republic for it to withdraw its support for the Spanish Royal family. Alfonso was forced to move to Rome, in 1933, where he took up residence in the Grand Hotel. Juan had travelled to England where he had enrolled in the British Navy.

Paco, his head still spinning with the shock, wrote an immediate reply to the Viscount saying it would be an honour to meet with the Prince and that he would certainly bring his bicycle. He sealed the letter and gave it to the hotel receptionist who said he would arrange for it to be delivered by hand.

The following afternoon, Paco, his head buzzing with excitement and anticipation, collected his bike from the Velodrome and headed for his rendezvous with the Prince. He pedalled along the busy streets, his heart pumping in his chest. He arrived at 228 Rue de Rivoli, the address of the prestigious Hotel Le Meurice, which lay between the Place de la Concorde and the Musée du Louvre, facing the Tuileries Garden.

The expression on the doorman's face told Paco that he was expected.

'Bonjour Monsieur Cepeda. Welcome to Le Meurice.'

Paco wheeled his bicycle under the arch, through the huge double doors and into the hotel reception. The interior was stunning. He had entered a gilded palace. Walking his bicycle across the gleaming marble floor, Paco suddenly felt very small and insignificant, but also a little conspicuous. It is not everyday someone appears in the foyer of a glamorous hotel with a racing bicycle. Beautiful chandeliers glistened from the ceiling and, looking around, Paco marvelled at the grand paintings and the tall columns, edged in gold leaf.

Next to the reception, stood a smartly dressed gentleman who introduced himself as the Viscount of Rocomora.

'Welcome Francisco. I am the Prince's secretary. Thank you for coming. The Prince is looking forward to meeting you and I see that you have brought your bicycle. Splendid. The Prince will be with us shortly.'

The Viscount led Paco to a comfortable sofa, where they waited for the Prince's entrance. Within a few minutes, the Prince appeared and strode towards Paco.

He was wearing a crisp, white, open-necked shirt and dark, neatly pressed trousers. He was an impressive man, tall and slim and he had a warm smile. He held out his hand in greeting.

'Thank you for coming at such short notice. It is an honour to meet you.'

'I can assure you that the honour is mine, your majesty,' replied Paco, bowing his head and shaking the Prince's hand firmly.

'And here is your bicycle. What an impressive machine. Now, how many kilometres is the race?'

'This year, the race is four thousand, three hundred and thirty-eight kilometres, your majesty. I try not to think of the length. I intend to take each stage as it comes.'

'That sounds very wise. And what are your ambitions for this year's competition?'

'To do my best, to make my family and my country proud of me and, God willing, to finish in Paris.'

'I am sure you will ride well. Now, I wonder if I would be able to ride this wonderful machine.'

'Of course, your majesty. Perhaps we should take the bike across the road to the Gardens.'

The three men left the hotel, crossed the street and entered the magnificent Tuileries Gardens through an imposing gate. The Esplanade des Feuillants stretched out before them towards the Louvre.

'This looks like the perfect spot,' said the Viscount.

Paco loosened the straps on the toe clips and handed the bike to the Prince.

'The bike is a little small for me but I will do my best not to fall off. I don't want to ruin your chances before you even start,' the Prince said with a laugh.

Paco watched, a little nervously, as the Prince pedalled off down the gravel esplanade. He looked a little ungainly with his knees protruding, not being able to straighten his long legs. He cycled down the path for about three hundred metres before he turned in a wide arc and returned, weaving in and out of some elegant couples who were promenading and enjoying the Parisian sunshine.

'That was splendid,' said the Viscount. 'Well done, your majesty. Perhaps you should enter next year's race.'

'I don't think so. It is a stunning machine but the saddle is not so comfortable.'

Everyone laughed.

'I'm glad I can return the bicycle to Señor Cepeda in one piece,' the Prince said with a smile.

'Thank you,' replied Paco, taking back his cherished bike.

'Well, we wish you the best of luck for tomorrow. We will be following your progress and I'm sure the people of Spain will also be supporting you.'

'I will do my best sir.'

Paco walked to the park gates with the Prince and the Viscount and the three men waited for a gap in the traffic before crossing the road to the hotel.

'Now after all that exercise you must join us for a drink. And don't worry, you can bring the bicycle with you,' said the Prince.

Paco was relieved. He did not want to let his precious bike out of his sight.

When the men had finished talking and it was time for Paco to go, the Prince and the Viscount walked him to the entrance.

'Good luck once again and thank you for taking the time to visit us.'

'It was an honour to meet you,' replied Paco.

Paco walked his bike to the road, turned and waved to the two men before pedalling off into the late afternoon sunshine. He could not stop smiling. Spanish Royalty had ridden his bike and his participation in the twenty-ninth Tour de France had now been given a Royal seal of approval. He could not wait to get back to the hotel to tell the other Spanish riders about his afternoon with the Prince of Asturias. The question was, would they ever believe him?

8

INSIDE THE TOUR

The Tour de France can be a lonely place for a Spanish rider, a long way from home and surrounded by foreign voices. Added to this, as Paco's French and English were limited to only a few words and phrases, establishing friendships was particularly difficult. Finding a real friend in this race is like finding treasure, he thought to himself.

On the other occasions he had ridden the race, Paco had been forced to use all his charm to win the respect of the Aces, particularly in the 1931 Tour when he was the only Spanish Ace competing. Another Spaniard, Salvador Cardona, started the race that year but as a touriste-routier. However, during the actual stages, no rider could really complain about being lonely. There was far too much happening, even when the peloton was ambling along at twenty-five kilometres per hour. Then there would be time for stories and jokes, when the language could become a little crude. This was something to which Paco never became accustomed. But he also knew and accepted that the peloton was the domain of males and machoism and bravado. Here, the riders could curse and swear to their heart's content, in the knowledge that their wives, girl-friends and children were safely out of earshot.

A bond amongst riders is always necessary, no more so than when the wind is blowing. Riding can be a torture without help from the peloton. Anyone who has ever ridden a bicycle, and especially those who have raced, will know that a stage into a strong headwind is the rider's worst enemy. There is no slope or speed more painful. It is difficult to find the right gear to enable meaningful progress, without sapping the strength and energy from your legs. To Paco, it was the toughest adversary. Give me a mountain climb, or the steepest and most technical descent, Paco would often think - anything but those long, tortuous flats into a brutal headwind. When faced with these strong headwinds, the riders had to organise themselves to reduce the violence of the wind. They did this by rotating the leader so that no one rider had to battle into the headwind for too long, and the group did not suffer from that invisible enemy. Even worse was the dreaded cross-wind which could split a large group of riders into several parts, each small group of riders working desperately to find some shelter, and also not wanting to lose touch with the group ahead or be dropped by the riders around them. If a gap opens it must be closed imme-diately, otherwise it grows, like a piece of elastic being stretched. When the elastic snaps the rider is done for. There is nothing more menacing or demoralising than seeing a group of riders disappear up the road, leaving an isolated rider to face the full force of the wind alone.

Paco's charm was one of his greatest assets on the Tour. His good sense of humour and his warm smile meant he was well liked by all the Aces, except for some issues that he had with Charles Pélissier. But then he was not alone in that respect. The Pélissier brothers had not always endeared them-selves either to the peloton or to Henri Desgrange. Paco was essentially a modest young man, whereas Charles Pélissier was something of a showman, hence his nickname or nicknames, the Elegant One, Valentino and Charles the Great. He also had a fashionable and attractive wife, with whom he often posed for photographs at the start or finish of stages. So Paco and Pélissier had very little or nothing in common. Paco was relatively poor, Pélissier was rich, Paco was humble, Pélissier was arrogant, Paco rode the Tour mainly for passion, Pélissier for money. Unsurprisingly, Charles Pélissier was not amongst Paco's closest friends.

Amongst the peloton in the 1931 Tour, the Frenchman, Jean Maréchal, and, the Belgian, Maurice De Waele, were probably his best friends and allies, but it was hard not to like Paco, with his happy-go-lucky spirit. Always talkative and good natured, he also stood out from the crowd as one of the smartest dressers. He was very stylish and always impeccably groomed. The Tour was, after all, an amazing carnival and Paco was determined to enjoy every moment of it. Just being part of this extravagant race was enough to give Paco goose-bumps every morning. He was grateful for the small stipend he received from the organisers to compete but, if truth be told, if he had not received a single franc in payment for riding the Tour, he would still have jumped at the opportunity of lining up at the start of the race in Paris.

His friendship with Maréchal, the Frenchman, developed more after the day's stage rather than on the road. During the stage, Maréchal, who was not one of the best French riders, had to work for his team. This meant that he often finished well down in the overall classification. In contrast, his friend-ship with the veteran, Maurice De Waele, was established on the road. De Waele had started his professional career in 1924 and by 1931 was riding his fourth Tour de France. He had been second in 1927, third in 1928 and in 1929 he had won it, in spite of falling ill during the race. His victory provoked that famous, disparaging, comment from Desgrange, 'We have a corpse for a winner,' but De Waele took it on the chin. He was a strong rider and Paco was grateful for his friendship. De Waele knew everything there was to know about racing at the top level. Belgians were hard riders. They could maintain incredible speeds on the flat and frequently trained and raced, day after day, through wind, rain and mud, not to mention over the hazardous cobbles. To the Spaniards, who were generally lighter and smaller, the long flat stages were something to be endured, so to have a Belgian as an ally was a blessing.

De Waele often came to Paco's rescue when the winds were wild. On these occasions, Paco would feel most isolated. When he suddenly found himself at the head of the pack, the chances were that nobody would move to the front to relieve him. But De Waele became his protector. Whenever the wind blew hard, he found Paco a place inside the echelon and refused to allow him to take the lead.

'Paco, my friend, if you want to make it to Paris, you must save your energy.'

'I was much obliged to him,' remarked Paco. 'If anyone does not know about cycling, he cannot imagine what an enemy the wind is, and I owe so much to De Waele. This Belgian was a true gentleman.

In that same Tour, like an orphan, Paco was adopted by the Australian-Swiss team.

'I was in such a bad condition from the start of the race. The first few days of the Tour are always brutal and so hard to prepare for. The flat stages are always fast and furious and this is when you are most in need of a team. I approached them and we formed a temporary unofficial international team, to which I contributed with all my effort, as any other team member would. In that way, we survived the first week. I rode better and so did they.'

Each race day, Paco followed the same routine. He would wake up two hours before the start and head straight for the massage therapist. He would usually share the services of a masseur with another rider to save money. The morning massage was imperative. The warm hands of the soigneur working away at the calves and thighs, easing the bruising and the aches and pains from the previous day and softening the muscles for the torture which lay ahead. Then, of course, there was the customary visit to the lavatory. The nerves were there from the moment he awoke, so this was never a problem. Paco was then given his jersey, a gleaming white cap, and clean bandages for the ankles and wrists, if the rider needed them, as well as several creams to ward-off the cold and the humidity on the legs. There were other balms to avoid annoying irritations like saddle sores, cuts and boils. Once these preliminaries were finished, the riders went to the restaurant to have breakfast. This was actually a complete meal. The menu included a purée, cooked ham, fried meat, grilled chicken with French fries or salad, fried eggs or an omelet, jam and fruits, all in generous portions. Finally, it was washed down with a beautiful bowl of coffee, into which Paco always poured butter. How he enjoyed it. The riders consumed so many calories during those breakfasts that no one suffered or felt faint in the first hundred kilometres of a stage.

Paco's teammate, Vicente Trueba was legendary for the amount of food that he could put away at breakfast. The tiny Spaniard, not only left his fellow riders gasping in the mountains, he also left them open-mouthed at the breakfast table. Vicente's nickname was the Flea of Torrelavega, as he weighed only forty-five kilograms. Nevertheless, he was usually the last rider to leave the table at breakfast and dinner. One evening, when all the riders had finished, only Vicente was left scraping the remains from his plate. When the waitress passed, she asked him if he was ready for dessert.

'Yes please,' he replied. 'I'll have ham, fried eggs and another steak and some more bread, please.'

José Bobillo, a member of the Cantabrian Federation, who was standing nearby, said to Trueba, 'You will have spent all your money before the end of the Tour if you eat so much.'

Trueba was given the normal fifty francs per day for his accommodation, food and repairs but he had already spent eighty francs for the repair of a crooked wheel the day before.

'Don't worry,' he replied. 'When we get to the mountains, I can win two thousand francs for being the first to the summit.'

After his morning meal, Paco would take his bike, which the mechanics had left ready in the racks, with whatever gears he had selected the night before. Every morning, the rider's bikes were always set out, chocked and perfectly neat, repaired and cleaned.

Paco then headed towards the signatures' control and then, after that, to the tables where he would pick up his supplies for the day's stage. Each day, Paco would take the same rations. Two boiled eggs, three rice cakes, one butter and ham sandwich and one jam sandwich, one box with twenty sugar cubes and a small pack with twelve prunes and four bananas. Additionally, there were two drums with mineral water, tea or coffee, whichever the rider preferred. Paco always opted for the water. When the stage was longer than two hundred and twenty kilometres, there were usually one or two additional supply controls along the way.

In every control area, at the start of a stage, a famous Paris outlet set up a mobile cafeteria at which the riders could have one or two expressos before they finally went to the start line.

Every stage had signature controls, in addition to the signature control at the start of the stage. This was to ensure there was no cheating. In earlier Tours, there had been infamous tales of riders taking short cuts and even getting on trains. In fact, the first Tour, in 1903, had been so plagued by cheating, Desgrange threatened to abandon plans for a second Tour. In the end, he relented but established an exhaustive rule book to keep the riders in check and lessen the opportunities for them to cut corners and destroy the credibility of the race. Some of the rules were necessary but many seemed unnecessarily harsh and drew the anger and protest of the riders.

The most famous protest in the Tour's history came from the Pélissier brothers in the 1924 Tour, when they refused to ride, abandoned the race on the third stage and launched a vitriolic attack on Desgrange and his rule book. Henri Pélissier took offence when commissaire, André Trialoux, at the start of the race in Cherbourg, without asking, lifted his jersey to check how many jerseys he was wearing. The rules stated that riders had to finish the stage wearing the same number of jerseys that they were wearing at the start of the stage. On cold mornings, Henri would often start wearing two and then discard one, during the stage, which was against the rules. Pélissier started the stage but, at Coutances, he persuaded his brother, Francis, and a teammate, Maurice Ville, to abandon. The brothers quit the Tour in protest and met with Albert Londres, a journalist from *Le Petit Parisien*, in a cafe. He took up their case and launched an attack on Desgrange and his Tour, accusing him of enslaving and humiliating the riders. His piece was called 'Les Forçats de la Route', the Convicts of the Road.

Pélissier was enraged. 'They wouldn't treat mules the way we're treated. We're not weaklings, but my God, they treat us so brutally. And if I so much as stick a newspaper under my jersey at the start, they check to see it's still there at the finish. One day, they'll start putting lumps of lead in our pockets because God made men too light.'

'You wouldn't believe that all this is about nothing more than a few jerseys. This morning, in Cherbourg, a race official came up to me and without a word, he pulled up my jersey to check that I'm not wearing two. What would you say if I pulled open your waistcoat to see if your shirt was clean? That's the way these people behave and I won't stand for it. That's what this is all about.'

'But what if you were wearing two jerseys?' asked Londres.

That's the point. If I want to, I can wear fifteen. What I can't do is start with two and finish with only one.'

'Why not?'

'Because that's the rule. We don't only have to work like donkeys, we have to freeze or suffocate as well. Apparently, that's an important part of the sport. So I went off to find Desgrange.'

'I can't throw my jersey on the road, then?' I asked Desgrange.

'No,' he said, 'You can't throw away anything provided by the organisation.'

'But this isn't the organisation's - it's mine.'

'I don't conduct arguments in the street,' Desgrange replied.

'OK,' I said, 'If you're not prepared to talk about it in the street, I'm going back to bed.'

'We'll sort it all out Brest,' he said.

'It will definitely be sorted out in Brest,' I said, 'Because I'm quitting. And I did.'

'You have no idea what the Tour de France is,' Henri said to Londres. 'It's a calvary. And what's more, the way to the cross only had fourteen stations — we've got fifteen. We suffer on the road. But do you want to see how we keep going? Wait...'

From his bag he took a phial. 'That, that's cocaine for our eyes and chloroform for our gums.'

'Here,' said Ville, tipping out the contents of his bag, 'Horse liniment to keep my knees warm. And pills? You want to see the pills?' They got out three boxes apiece.

'In short,' said Francis, 'We run on dynamite.'

Years later, when Paco was racing, there were still plenty of reasons for the riders to gripe and grumble and the signature control was one of them. Not all the controls were compulsory and, to universal annoyance, the riders were only told which ones would be compulsory just before the departure each morning. Once the Aces were lined up at the front of the race, Monsieur Cazalis, the starter, announced which controls needed 'signature obligatoire', compulsory signature. These stations were something to behold. Paco remembered his first experience very clearly. How could he forget it?

'We always approached the first control point at a terrific speed.' Paco wrote in an article for his fans in *Excelsior*. 'There were usually thirty or forty of us in a group. As we approached the tables, caps and goggles were ripped from our heads. Every rider needed to sign the sheet, otherwise, there would be a sanction. Monsieur Desgrange loved his sanctions. It was a dreadful situation. The riders dropped their machines and jumped to the jury's desk, where many pencils were available. But the dirty tricks started almost at once. The first ones to arrive at the tables and sign broke the sharp lead points, before heading back for their bikes. This was to gain a small advantage on those left queuing to sign. Confusion followed. Some riders lost as much as two minutes waiting for their pencil to be sharpened. Meanwhile, the perpetrators had already escaped, their trails and their wicked grins hidden in clouds of dust.'

In his first Tour, Paco had been the victim of these dirty schemes more than once, so he made sure that, when Monsieur Cazalis announced the number of compulsory stations, he asked the attendants for extra pencils and they quickly provided him with some. He felt more comfortable once he had some pencils stuffed in his jersey pocket. On one occasion, an attendant gave him an attractive fountain pen. Paco thanked him. It was a nice gesture but useless for the required signature.

Each time Paco arrived at a control point, he became more

practised and skilful at the art of signing in. Some riders, in their eagerness to save time, threw their bikes to the ground and made straight for the tables, but Paco always picked out a marshal or spectator and asked him to hold his bike. Then he searched among the list of riders for the box with his race number. There was always a lot of pushing and shoving, as well a some colourful language at the table. It was almost impossible to keep your hand steady but once signed in, Paco took his bicycle calmly from the attendant, thanked him and headed towards the road, not forgetting of course to safely stow his pencil in his pocket, ready for the next control.

Avoiding the chaos at the controls was vital. Sometimes when the riders tried to reclaim their bikes, many of them found they were hidden beneath a pile of iron tubes, so they lost valuable time disentangling them. Sometimes riders were in such a rush and so distracted that they took the wrong bike, even though each bike bore a different race number.

In the 1931 Tour, the national teams started ten minutes in front of the touristes-routiers in a number of stages. As a consequence of these battles at the control points, the stages often started very fast. The Aces would set off at a speed of forty or forty-five kilometres per hour and those like Paco, who started at the back of the main group of favourites, could quickly lose one or two minutes. When that happened, they could forget about ever catching them. Paco was very conscious about being left behind at the start or at the control stations. If you lost contact with your teammates or your friends, then you could be within the reach of the forty or so touristes-routiers, and none of the top riders wanted to face the shame of being caught by a touriste-routier. The touristes-routiers were either divided into regional teams or rode as individuals. There were a few very good riders amongst this group but, on the whole, they were riding in a different race. The organisers lived in fear of a touriste-routier winning a stage, never mind the race. In the 1931 Tour, the Austrian, Max Bulla gave everyone a scare when he quickly made up the ten minute deficit and stormed into the lead on stage two. He held on to win the stage and became the only touriste-routier to lead the Tour. He went on to win two more stages that year, one in the mountains. Although two other stages were won by touristes-routiers that year, it was very unlikely that a rider from this group would ever win the Tour.

To avoid losing time at the control points, riders would always try to find a loophole. In some groups, there was a rider who signed for the rest of the group. Within all the mess, the hurrying and the scrambling towards the tables, nobody in the jury could verify which riders had signed and which had not, and all of them at least made the gesture of getting close to the desk. In this way, the teams could favour their leaders. The organisation looked down on this kind of behaviour and, if caught, the riders would receive a sanction, but some riders were very skilled at the control table and, when the rules needed to be broken, in Paco's opinion, the French and the Italians were the true masters of this dark art.

When the riders approached the mountains, another important decision to be made was when to change gear. Although derailleurs were allowed in some races, Desgrange would not allow them to be used in the Tour. He did not want to make the racing any easier for the riders. Instead, the riders had gears on both sides of the rear hub. The bikes had big fork ends at the back to accommodate the two sprockets on each side of the hub. In the mountains, riders favoured twenty-two and twenty-four teeth on the sprockets on one side and twenty and eighteen on the other. The front chainring usually had forty-two or forty-four teeth. On the flat stages, riders would change to fifty teeth on the front chainring and sixteen and seventeen and nineteen and twenty teeth on the rear cogs. Flexibility was the key. You had to know exactly when to change gears. Some riders would go as far as they could up the hill before changing gear, while others would change at the bottom of the hill. Paco's teammate Vicente Trueba, despite his diminutive stature, would often stay in the same gear for the entire climb, riding much of it out of the saddle.

You could easily be dropped if you did not change gear at the right time. Sometimes if the peloton saw one of the better riders stop to change a wheel, they would ride on at top speed and leave him to chase on his own. It paid to know the course well. The riders were always looking for ways to gain an advantage. Sometimes a rider, who knew the course well, would bluff that he was stopping to change into a higher gear when, knowing that there was a steep hill coming up, he actually stayed in the same low gear. When the riders remounted, those who had changed to a higher gear were in for a shock. When the incline came, they either had to stop to change their wheel again or grind their way up the climb, zig-zagging across the road. Either way, the fraudster had disappeared from view.

Paco was, above all, an honest rider. If he won a race, it mattered to him that he had won it fairly. He knew that cheating of one kind or another was common throughout the peloton but he disapproved of it strongly. He absolutely loved this sport and the competition but had to resign himself to defeat if he was beaten by someone who had cheated. What else could he do? All he could do was remain true to himself. However, on burning hot days, when the riders thought that they might die of thirst, even Paco's resolve was tested. When their water bottles were bone dry and with no feed station in sight, the riders became demented by thirst. They would stop in villages and towns and raid bars and grocery stores, desperate for a drink. Thirst was a treacherous enemy that destroyed you. Paco remembered that on the hottest, driest, dustiest days, you felt like you were being strangled. The torment was unbearable. Once your two bidons were empty, thirst provoked both mental and physical anxiety and, when exhaustion set in, the body began to fade. Beers, lemonades, brandy, anything, as long as it smelt like liquid, was found. The cafes, bars and hotels all came under attack as the riders passed through the towns and villages. A rider who was off the back of the group and arrived late was forced to descend into the cellar in order to find something to quench his thirst. He would seize what he could, drink it, and leave as fast as he could. He has no money. He cannot pay. He grabs his bike and sprints up the road like a madman. Once, Paco was riding in a group with Joseph Mauclair, the Frenchman, who led a guerilla-style attack on a bar.

'Paco, you go into the bar and ask for a bottle of beer. Entertain the boss with a story. Meanwhile, we will slip inside and take what we can.'

Paco could not deny that he had joined in the raid and he was not proud of the part he had played, but, like the others, he was delirious with thirst.

In Paco's second Tour, dramatic changes in the weather made some of the stages almost impossible. Heavy rain in the Pyrenees turned roads to mud. On the Aubisque and the Tourmalet, he had to get off numerous times to remove mud which had clogged his wheels. Another time, he had to walk because a landslide had removed half of the road and it was better to be cautious rather than be bold and then slip and fall to an untimely death. When it rained in the mountains, it was usually a deluge and icy cold. The roads were narrow and covered in gravel, stones and rocks. The sky was dark, an imposing black. To be alone or suffer a puncture or a mechanical failure in a place like that was a nightmare. The stones and the mud increased the likelihood. But in spite of all the drawbacks, it was better to keep riding rather than stop. Everyone had bad luck. The first time Paco punctured, he was lucky that he was on an easy stretch of road. He fixed it quickly and was soon back in contact with his group. The second time, he was not so fortunate. How sad he was to see the peloton disappear. He feared for himself; he was alone. Slipping and falling in the mud, he tore his raincoat and his jersey. His strength and resolve were sorely tested. It was minus two degrees on the mountain. When he made it to the valley, it was thirty degrees above zero, in the shade. How the riders suffered on these days. When the sun hit their faces, that had been spattered in mud for one hundred and fifty kilometres, they were left with cement masks. They were unrecognisable.

Paco Cepeda felt that he had little in common with other professional cyclists. First and foremost, he did not consider himself to be a true professional rider. Most of the full-time professionals, who made up only a third of the field each year in the Tour, raced, not because they loved to ride, but because of the small fortune that could be made from winning.

Antonin Magne was a case in point. He was a farmer and the son of a peasant from Cantal. As a young boy, he used to roll a massive rock in his garden to build up his strength and train himself to endure suffering and pain. As a young man, he still went to bed at eight in the evening and was then up on cold, dark, winter mornings to milk his cows. After that, he would ride through the frosted or freezing countryside, calculating in his mind the number of francs he would earn when he won the Tour, how many cows his winnings would buy him and how much milk they would yield. He would go to the foot of the Col d'Aubisque and ride it fifty times in training so that he knew every twist and turn of the road and where the road surface was particularly bad. He would work out which were the best gears to use and where was the best place to attack his rivals. Then on the day of the stage, he would win it with time to spare. He told Desgrange that he would win the Tour twice, which is exactly what he did in 1931 and 1934. In 1931, he was the only rider who knew of a recently paved descent, so he chose a big gear to gain an advantage on his rivals, riding into Luchon twenty-eight minutes and forty seconds ahead of André Leducq, the winner of the Tour the previous year. Most of the riders, and Desgrange, considered Magne to be dull and serious. His nickname was the Monk or Tonin the Wise. He rarely smiled or shared a joke and he was seldom seen at gatherings or parties. He disliked the press and hardly ever gave them headlines. Stoical best sums him up. He only drank water and lived by his motto, with which he signed off all his letters; 'There is no glory without virtue.'

PART THREE

ONE LAST TOUR

The Twenty-Ninth Tour de France, 1935

9

THE GRAND DÉPART

July 4th, Stage 1, Paris to Lille, 262 kilometres, (35.41kph)

T he opening day of the Tour de France is like no other opening day of any stage race in the world. Excitement grips the streets of Paris. On the fourth of July, 1935, crowds, predominantly French, gathered in their thousands to support their national team, led by André Leducq and Antonin Magne. These two men, both former winners of the race, were admired and respected for their achievements and were held in awe by the young boys, in short trousers and flat caps, who wedged themselves between the elbows and knees of their heroes at the photo call. These men of steel would, over the next month, eat up the kilometres around France and suffer horribly in the mountains. Their faces, smiling now, would soon be clenched and tortured. Along with their fellow riders, they would endure the heat, the rain, the dust, the thirst and many, many pitfalls along, what would feel like, an endless road.

In the courtyard of the offices of *L'Auto*, where the riders would traditionally congregate before the start of the race, the intensity was noticeable. In the 1935 Tour, there were more riders than in previous years and the organisers had introduced a new innovation, a barrier, behind which the riders were protected and less exposed to the enthusiasm of their fans. Most of the riders were there but the Italian Aces had yet to appear. Perhaps they were still at breakfast, as they had a reputation for eating more than their fair share, which might have been the reason for the slow starts they often made in races.

Lucien Cazalis, sat at his control table, where the riders signed on before each stage. Alongside him sat the imposing race director Monsieur Desgrange. Monsieur Cazalis was in a panic as the slots for the Italian riders remained blank, without signatures.

'Where are my Italians?' he cried. 'I need my Italians. Where are my Italians?' His voice thundered above the hubbub of the crowd. He continued to bellow, 'Martano! Bergamaschi!' in his best Italian accent, that he had cultivated on his frequent visits to the other side of the Alps to sign up an Italian team.

Most of the riders were pensive. Only Leducq was smiling, living up to his nickname, 'Joyeau Dede'. Otherwise, the riders remained tight-lipped. The journalists hovered, curious and eager to catch a final word or a fragment of a conversation. The parents of some of the riders looked a little tense. Madame Lapébie, the mother of the French brothers Roger and Guy, showed the usual emotion at these starts, despite the fact that Guy was not riding this year. Nevertheless, her thought was the same as it always was; hope that this year's Tour de France would pass without an accident for Roger.

Among the crowds, along the sidewalks of the district of Montmartre, everyone was waiting for the great procession to begin. Paco was dreading this opening stage. It would be fast and frantic all the way to Lille and then they would be heading towards the dreaded and murderous 'pave' of the North. He had ridden the famous cobbles before but he still felt like he was going into the unknown. Yes, he had been in training for a few months, but, this year, he was riding as an individual, without the backing of a team. All the National teams would be riding hard from the start, to put their captains into the lead. In the past, these flat stages were considered to be a period of preparation for the mountains, but now they were fiercely contested. This would be the case today, particularly in the latter part of the stage, which followed the same profile as the famous classic race, Paris-Roubaix.

The riders edged their bikes forward. The eager touristes-routers had advanced on the experienced riders, the Aces and the Individuals. Most of them were unknowns and the crowds were scanning their newspapers where the riders numbers and names were displayed. Dante Gianello, from Cannes, cheekily snuck up and took a spot right on the front line. The riders stood still. There was no more time to dream. The engines of the following cars were running and the journalists had put away their notepads. Only the radio reporters continued to chatter.

Finally, the peloton was called to order and the final count-down began. A few riders tried to laugh or share a joke, to appear casual, but even the veterans, the seasoned riders, felt their hearts leap and tighten. The first-timers and the younger touristes-routiers looked nervous and pre-occupied. The final seconds ticked away. The clock on the Place de la Madeleine was at seven twenty-one, and to a rising roar, a sudden pistol shot stirred the riders into action. The first turns of the pedals carried the riders into a wave of movement along the rue de la Orange-Batelière, rue Drouot, les Grande Boulevards, rue Royale and the place de la Concord. The Belgian team was at the front, and behind the competitors, hundreds of young enthusiasts, for a brief moment, dared to dream, along with their heroes, as they rode at the back of the peloton. The thick, dark cloud of riders made its way towards avenue des Champs-Elysées and the iconic Arc de Triomphe. The Champs-Elysées was designed for grand parades, with its vast pavements and wide streets, and it was still filled with enormous crowds, three or four deep. They had come from every part of France. As the riders processed through this neutralised section, they were flanked on either side by the cyclards, the bicycle mounted police, who provided an impressive escort to these 'géants de la route'. The crowds waved their hands and hats and shouted and cheered.

'Courage!' 'Allez les gars!' 'Bravo!' 'Attention de ne pas tomber.'

Sadly, much to their frustration, many of the eager young fans could not ride with the stars for very long, as they had to be back at their workplaces. They went as far as they could but, eventually, they had to resign themselves to leaving this spectacular peloton, by turning off up a side street.

To add to all the chaos, a young man, hanging from the running board of a car, handed out Tour de France specials. These were greedily grabbed by the spectators and even one or two of the lesser known riders, who, no doubt, wanted to know who they were riding with. The Champs-Elysées, the place de l'Etoile and the avenue de la Grande-Armée, would be the riders' last view of the capital, before they set out on their epic journey.

Vésinet was the official start of the race and all the riders came to a standstill there. In the shade of the trees, there was the usual struggle as the crowd tried to get one last glimpse of their favourite riders. As for the riders, there was the inevitable emotion, even for the experienced ones. Charles Pélissier's wife gave her husband a final passionate embrace and more than a few kisses, to a chorus of whistles from some of the other riders. Finally, they gathered themselves for the traditional line-up in front of a mass of photographers. There was one exception. The Italian, Raffaele Di Paco, arrived smiling and well groomed after all the photographs had been taken.

There was a delay of twenty-five minutes before the starter prepared to drop the flag. The crowd stretched and strained, trying to match faces to bib numbers. Of the ninety-three starters, forty-four were first timers and mostly unknown to the spectators. Others of course were very familiar to the Parisiennes. There was the confident looking Belgian team. Romain Maes and Félicien Vervaecke had both talked about winning this year's race. The curly-headed Italian, Giuseppe Martano, was easily picked out, alongside Vasco Bergamaschi who was looking a little bewildered. Next in line was the rugged Francesco Camusso and then the tall and elegant Di Paco. The Spanish had fielded a team of climbers, led by the tiny Trueba and Ezquerra, with Cañardo as their rouler. Four of the team, Antonio Prior, Emiliano Alvarez, Cipriano Elys and Isidio Figueras, were new to the Tour and then there was the experienced Salvador Cardona, the first Spaniard ever to win a stage in the Tour de France. As an individual Spanish rider, Paco did not line up with the Spanish team but he found a place just behind his compatriots.

Four years earlier, at the start of the twenty-fifth Tour de France, Paco had actually found himself starting at the front of race, owing to a curious mistake made by the usually reliable Monsieur Cazalis. Paco could remember it quite vividly. It was when the roll call was being taken.

'Number one, Alfred Haemerlinck. Number two, Gaston Rebry,' Mr Cazalis called, until the five teams with their forty riders had all been named. Now it is my turn thought Paco. Number 41, he said quietly to himself. But no announcement came.

Mr Cazalis then continued, 'Touriste-routier Number 101,'

and so on, until the forty touristes-routiers had also been named.

Paco remembered feeling slightly stunned at the end of the roll call. When his name had not been announced, his eyesight went blurry, he felt a lump in his throat and he thought that he was about to cry.

'What about Cepeda?' shouted a Spanish journalist from the crowd.

Monsieur Cazalis threw up his arms and came over to Paco. He begged his forgiveness and then ushered Paco ahead of all the other riders and asked the photographers to take some pictures of him. To Paco, it felt like a hundred photographs were taken. And that was how in 1931, Paco found himself leading the Tour de France, at least for a few wheel revolutions.

This year, as in the previous five years, since the introduction of the national teams, the French team was the strongest. It was led by Antonin Magne. He stood out with his beautiful new, white cap and his eyes suggested he was a man with a mission. Leducq was still smiling and joking. Sponsored by Alcyon-Dunlop, the most powerful and dominant team at the time, and a Tour winner, he was the complete opposite to Magne. A Parisian and a bit of a rascal, he charmed everyone with his cheeky grin and good looks. Next to him, Maurice Archambaud still bore the black eye that he had sustained in a recent fall at the French Championships. René Le Grevès and René Vietto stood coldly and resolutely beside their bikes. Vietto looked determined and thoughtful. Paco nervously checked his back pockets to see if he had forgotten anything. At the last minute, before the flag was dropped and the lead car departed, Georges Speicher had everyone laughing as he ran up and down looking for his two spare tyres which he had almost forgotten.

'My tubes. Who has stolen my tubes?' he cried, pointing an

accusing finger at Le Grevès. 'If it's you, Breton, I'll turn your bed upside down tonight.'

For the newcomers, this was the time to look around in amazement and take in the atmosphere in their first Tour de France. In order to have the best view when Biscot dropped the flag, the die-hard fans had arrived in the very early hours of the morning. They had taken up their positions on the grass but whether through tiredness or too much wine, several of them were asleep. They would miss the start altogether.

Finally, the flag was dropped and the twenty-ninth Tour de France was under way. The start was steady enough and the first test was the cote du Pecq, a gentle leg stretcher for the riders, but nothing compared to what would await them later in the week. The peloton began to stretch out in single file as it climbed, at a moderate pace.

It wasn't long before the main bunch was stirred by Merviel, Vervaecke, Bergamaschi and Benoît Faure. Speicher was the first to be dropped, being left behind with a puncture, at Conflans. At Beauvais, the crowds crammed into the streets, which were spectacularly decorated with colourful flags. People went to extraordinary lengths to catch a glimpse of the riders, hanging out of windows, standing on walls and hoisting children onto their shoulders. The peloton, with the German team at the front, raced across the cobbles, in pursuit of a breakaway which had passed through the packed streets a minute earlier, to deafening cheers.

The first feed station came at Amiens and there was the usual scrum. A sea of white caps bobbing and jostling to find a place at the table. After Amiens, came the tree-lined cote de Doullens, on the edge of the mining country. Here, the race suddenly kicked off, with the kind of ferocity that is normally seen in races in the north. It started with Jean Aerts, Edgard de Clauwe and Charles Pélissier. But the most destructive attack came from the twenty-two-year-old Belgian, Romain Maes.

Henri Desgrange described him as a 'compact ball of muscle'. Hunched over his bike, with his shoulders rolling, he was like a man possessed by the devil. His fiery eyes were fixed on the coal-coloured pave. One mistake and his front wheel could lodge itself in one of the huge gaps between the cobbles and he would come crashing down, like he had done the previous year. Maes's attack came in the heart of the mining town of Bruay-en-Artois. Its sinkholes were covered with crowds of fanatical spectators, waving and shouting. It was not long before he was two minutes ahead of a panic-stricken peloton, which soon split, with eight more riders going clear in pursuit of the stocky Belgian. Antonin Magne led De Caluwé, Le Grevès, Aerts, Jozef Moerenhout, and also Pélissier, René Debenne and François Neuville in the chase to bring back Maes..

Paco was merely a spectator on the opening day. Dreading this stage from the outset, like his fellow Spaniards, including the Aces, he now found himself slipping rapidly towards the back of a fragmenting peloton. The cheering of the crowds massed along the Champs-Élysées was now a distant memory. His Tour de France was rapidly unravelling before his eyes and he felt utterly powerless to do anything about it. He tried to hold his nerve but it was difficult. A lot of the touristes-routiers, the amateurs in this race, were ahead of him. His only consolation was that most of the Spanish Aces were around him, struggling to maintain the blistering pace set by the Belgian and French riders, through this bleak landscape of coal dust, dirt and cobbles.

The real drama of the day began when Maes arrived at the railway crossing at Niveau d'Haubourdin. The road gate had closed but the train had not yet arrived. To the astonishment of the crowd of working men and young boys who had gathered there, Maes spotted a small, open gate and, without dismounting, crossed the railway tracks. There were gasps of amazement from the onlookers. His pursuers were not so lucky. When the breakaway of four arrived, which included Pélissier, a freight train was passing at snail's pace. Panic followed.

'Watch out! Slow down!' shouted a large, working man with a bushy moustache. His outstretched arm reached towards Pélissier who was hurtling towards the barrier.

Pélissier came to a halt, while the other riders behind him mounted the pavement, as cars were already queuing at the barrier, blocking the road. The train seemed to take forever to pass and the four riders were trapped. Soon other riders would be arriving and their advantage would be lost. Even worse, Maes was gaining valuable seconds, maybe minutes, on them. They waited anxiously at the crossing. This was a disaster, but all the riders could do was swear at the trucks as they slowly rumbled past.

Finally, the last truck trundled past but even now the gate remained firmly shut. More confusion and cursing followed, until Magne noticed the smaller gate, the one through which Maes had passed a few minutes earlier. Magne made a beeline for it and the others followed. Next came the mass of riders and following cars and motorcycles which now clogged the road. The crossing was still barred, inexplicably. This was turning into a farce and the crowd which had initially been stunned by what they had witnessed were now beginning to see the funny side of the situation. Riders were weaving their bikes between the stationary vehicles and some were getting entangled with each other as they tried to squeeze through the same small gaps. Unsurprisingly, the riders were not laughing and there was was much pointing, waving, cursing and shaking of fists.

Paco arrived after the main peloton and found himself at the back of what seemed like an endless line of cars and people. Ahead, he could see riders had dismounted and were weaving between the cars and the spectators. He wondered what was happening. He dismounted and made slow progress towards what he assumed was the blockage.

Meanwhile, Maes was on a section of familiar cobblestones not far from his home, near Bruges. His quick thinking at the crossing had given him a crucial advantage and he was not about to give it up. He increased his pace as he approached Lille, the French capital of Flanders. Maes had, from a young age, worked in a brickyard, to provide for his family, so he knew what it was like to suffer. He arrived at the course of Croisé-Laroche, a minute clear of his four rivals, De Caluwé, Pélissier, Aerts and Magne. It was an emphatic victory for him and for Belgium, made all the more convincing when Leducq crossed the line a further two minutes back. There were considerable distances between the winner of the yellow jersey and the other favourites. The absurdity at the crossing and the terrible cobbles had taken their toll on some of the best riders. Merviel and Speicher finished four minutes down, Archambaud six, Bergamaschi seven, Di Paco eleven, Remo Bertoni lost fifteen minutes on the leader and Vietto and Camusso nineteen. But it was a dreadful day for the Spanish team. Trueba and Ezquerra toiled in, losing thirty-four minutes and a miserable looking Paco, blackened with coal dust, like a miner, crawled home in second to last place. He limped across the line eighty-ninth of the ninety-three starters. There had been three abandonments. Paco was just grateful he hadn't been among them.

This was going to be a testing Tour. At the end of the stage, Paco's sense of isolation hit home. In his first Tour he'd had the full support of the Spanish team and he had thrived. However, he had failed to finish his next two Tours, when he was riding alone, and here he was, in his fourth Tour, riding alone again and suffering. Maybe his father had been right. Maybe he was deluded in thinking that he could recapture the form of earlier years. So many negative thoughts tormented his mind and there was nobody he could turn to for encouragement, to distract him from those worries. To survive the first few punishing stages Paco would need to draw on all his experience and that unyielding Basque spirit.

Results of Stage 1

Winner: R. Maes, 7h. 23' 58"
F. Cepeda, 89th, 7h. 59' 55"

Overall: R. Maes, 7h. 23' 58"
F. Cepeda, 89th, 7h. 59' 55"

10

THE HELL OF THE NORTH

July 5th, Stage 2, Lille to Charleville, 192 kilometres,
(34.667 kph)

P aco woke the following morning stiff and sore. His bruised and aching body would recover but finishing second to last, on the opening stage, had hurt his pride and that would take a little longer to heal.

Traditionally, the riders woke two hours before the start of the stage. Paco made his way to the massage therapist and received a gentle massage. Feeling a little more like himself, he went to the hotel restaurant for breakfast, where he ate some grilled chicken with fries and an omelette. There was not a great deal of conversation at the breakfast table. Most of the riders were thinking about the day ahead.

Paco headed to the bike store to collect his bike. The dust and mud from the previous day's stage had gone and it looked as good as it had when he first saw it in Paris. He went through his ritual of checking it carefully. The mechanics were very good and he trusted them but this was something that he did, not solely out of habit, but because he enjoyed it. Since he was a boy, he had loved tinkering with his bike. He would often dismantle it, clean it thoroughly and then reassemble it with the bearings greased and the chain cleaned and freshly oiled so that it ran smoothly and silently. He could not stand the slightest rubbing or scraping noise.

Finally, he made his way towards the signatures' control and then to the food tables to pick up his supplies for the day. As always, he took his two boiled eggs, three cream cakes, a butter and ham sandwich and a jam sandwich, his box of twenty sugar cubes, a small pack with twelve prunes and four bananas. This sizeable stash of food was put into the pockets on his jersey which were to the front and the back. He headed over to the drums of water and filled up his two bidons. He pushed the cork stoppers down firmly so that they would not leak when the bike was bounced around on the murderous cobbles later that day. When he was sure that he had everything he needed for the day's stage, he made his way to the coffee house for his two espressos.

If Paco was hoping for some respite on the second day, those hopes rapidly diminished with the route taking in more hard and dangerous cobbled roads. It was Pélissier who drove the bunch on towards Valenciennes, before finally breaking away with a small group which, to Paco's surprise, included his friend Trueba. There was some relief in seeing this little group disappear up the road. The cobbles from Lille to Maubeuge, that is to say eighty-five kilometres, were more formidable than the day before. It was a lottery. These roads were nothing more than cattle tracks, centuries old deformed roads, constructed with misshapen cobble stones. This was the road to Hell where the merciless process of whittling down the field began. For a while, Paco would ride in single file on the very edge of the road to avoid the cobbles, but the gutters were, more often than not, filled with debris and so it would not be long before the line of riders found their way back onto the cobbles. Paco could feel his bike rattling beneath him. Every bone in his body vibrated and shook. This was a place of torture, torment and, invariably, drama.

There were punctures galore. The race leader, Maes, had three, and at one point was several minutes adrift of the main field. Thankfully for him, his Belgian teammates rallied around him and were strong enough to pace him back to the main pack. Why so many punctures? The new, metal, duralumin rims, which the riders had been moaning about the previous evening, kept the wheels so rigid that they made strange and sudden jumps on the deformed cobblestones. When the riders looked for some relief from the bone-shaking cobbles, by hopping their bikes onto the pavements, the clinker bricks that covered them hid debris that tore into even the most resistant tyre. The tyres, again supplied by the organisation, were glued to the metal rims with Chatterton compound. In the heat of the day, the adhesive, fixing the tyres to the rims, often began to melt, allowing the tyres to move on the rim and rotate. This made them more prone to punctures or even sliding off the rim altogether. It seemed to Paco that every ten metres a rider was on his bent knees on the grass verge, with his wheel wedged in his midriff and his hands desperately straining to prise off the tyre.

The riders had already become so practised in replacing tyres they had made an art of it, removing a spare from their chests and passing it over their heads in one broad movement. Paco counted himself lucky in only puncturing twice compared to Speicher who had punctured four times and Archambaud who had punctured on six occasions. Speicher was particularly unlucky as, at one point, there was no support vehicle nearby, so he had to join the touristes-routiers and find a bike shop where he could buy some tubulars. Leducq punctured three times and broke a wheel and Lapébie fell quite badly and injured his knee and broke his frame. Aerts and Louis Hardiquest were also fallers and Magne was knocked over by a spectator at a cross roads. This was crazy, thought Paco. How can anyone race under such intolerable conditions? Incredibly, no one had ever died racing the Tour de France but, in a day of spectacular crashes, it seemed only a matter of time before a rider lost their life. You needed more than strength, courage and heroism on days like this. You also needed a large slice of luck.

It had been another dramatic day, but Paco had to wait until supper to hear the full story. He rode for much of the day in small groups or alone, soft pedalling at times, longing for the finish line and counting down the kilometres. He came home in fifty-fifth place, with Sezney Leroux, a touriste-routier from France. One crumb of comfort was that his ride was an improvement on the opening stage but, the first two days of racing, had made him realise how unprepared he was for this challenge. Over four hundred and fifty kilometres had been covered in the first two days. Some of his weekly training rides, in the months before the Tour, had not amounted to as many kilometres. Had he bitten off more than he could chew?

It would have been easy to lose heart but Paco was made of sterner stuff. Having completed the Tour in 1930, he knew how infernal the pace could be in the opening week and he also knew that, if he could hold his nerve, and not panic, that he would grow in strength and that he could ride himself into this race. If he could survive until the roads began to rise, then the pace would drop and he would come into his own.

His body ached with pain and stiffness but the cobblestones

were over and, hopefully, when he went to bed that night, he would not be dreaming of them. He lay for a moment on his bed and thought of home, of his mother and father, his brothers and his sister, little Espe, and, of course, Teresa in Bilbao. They would be anxious for him, knowing that he had not come to this Tour at the peak of his physical fitness. He had promised he would keep them informed of his progress, so he took up his pen and wrote a few lines on the back of a postcard.

> *Charleville, 6 July 1935*
> *Dear Parents,*
>   *A little bit upset after these extremely hard stages of 'pave'. I am writing to you from this beautiful city, very historic from the times of the European war. I am still getting better and more motivated. Let's see later on.*
>   *On day 3, I met the King's son. I talked to him for one hour, he rode my bike, he is very unaffected and amusing. He was very thankful for the visit. That's all. Give my regards to everybody, and I am sending you, with Espe's company, my best regards.*
>   *Paco*

It was amazing how much you could get on the back of a postcard thought Paco. He looked at the words as they became more tightly packed towards the bottom of the card, as he read it over before placing it on his bedside table. He would leave it at the reception on his way to breakfast. He switched off the light and, still thinking of his family, back in Sopuerta, fell into a deep sleep.

Results of Stage 2

Winner: C. Pélissier, 5h. 32' 18"
F. Cepeda, 55th, 5h. 53' 08"

Overall: R. Maes, 12h. 53' 53"
F. Cepeda, 81st, 13h. 53' 03"

11

RECOVERY RIDE

July 6th, Stage 3, Charleville to Metz, 161 km, (35.9kph)

To Paco's relief, and to the relief of many of the other individuals and touristes-routiers, the pace eased on stage three. It was no surprise, following the relentless riding on the brutal, cobblestone roads of the first two stages. Paco's whole body ached and his legs felt swollen and bloated. Luckily, he had not fallen but there were many other casualties, sporting bandages on their knees and elbows. Again, there had been an astonishing number of punctures, many caused by nails, according to the newspapers, but talk at breakfast again revolved around the duralumin rims. They were not popular with the riders but who was prepared to challenge Monsieur Desgrange?

It seemed to Paco that the crowds had been larger than in his previous tours. This was partly owing to the expectation that Magne would ride to another victory for France but also largely on account of the Caravan which now preceded the race, showering the waiting spectators with sweets, cheeses, biscuits and paper hats. This year, there were more vehicles in the Caravan than ever. Forty-six different businesses were represented, offering a variety of products from chocolate by Menier, processed cheese from La Vache Qui Rit, and toasted bread from Biscottes, to name but a few.

After the two days of mad racing, the riders had a right to take a rest, although Henri Desgrange was probably quietly seething from the seat of his car, as he followed the action or lack thereof. The Charleville to Metz stage, with its flat roads and picturesque landscapes seemed like the stage for relaxation and recovery and where any thoughts of abandonment could be put aside. The peloton steadily made its way through Lorraine, with its green, neatly-marked fields and its sparkling rivers which flowed gently under a bright sun. It was a relaxing ride during the first two thirds of the stage and it provided an opportunity for the riders who were new to the Tour to make some acquaintances, and for old friends to reacquaint themselves. Such informalities had been impossible since Paris, the racing had been so hard. As the peloton ambled along, for the first time, it seemed that everyone was able to fully take in what it felt like to be part of this Tour.

It was only around Pierrepont, about fifty kilometres before the finish, that the race became energised. It began quite unexpectedly and came from the Italian, Bertoni. The peloton was suddenly split, with a handful of riders breaking clear. After twenty kilometres of chasing, most of the peloton managed to come back together and everyone thought that the finish was going to be played out by the Aces in a bunch sprint. But no sooner had the race come back together, the chasers sat up and stopped riding and this enabled Archambaud to steal away. Unfortunately, he could not stop Gustave Danneels from jumping on his wheel and, a little later, the specialist sprinter, Di Paco, joined them. The Italian had cleverly used some of the following cars to bring him up to the leaders, by riding in their slipstream. So, for Archambaud, all his hard work was wasted. As soon as Di Paco joined him, he knew that he would be the loser in a sprint. And so it was. The Frenchman was quickly distanced by the Belgian and the Italian. These two riders went thirty metres clear, before the cheering crowds which lined the finish, four or five deep, on boulevard Poincaré. Enjoying the warm, Saturday afternoon sunshine, heads craning in the direction of the three riders, they cheered loudly. At the finish line, Danneels could not hold off the fast finishing Italian, Di Paco, who used all his experience and form from previous years to win the stage by half a bike length.

The big peloton arrived one minute and thirty seconds later, with all the stars of the race, so the general classification remained unchanged, with Romain Maes keeping his hold on the yellow jersey.

Paco had a better day, finishing in sixty-second place, eight minutes behind the leader. He crossed the line in a small group made up by Georges Lachat, Ferdi Ickes, Benoît Faure and Trueba. Paco felt he was moving in the right direction, finishing higher up the field each day and improving his standing in the overall classification. As sorry as he had felt for himself after the first two stages, he had still had much better luck than poor Vietto. The much-loved French star had suffered more than his fair share of punctures, and then he had arrived in Charleville, at the end of stage two, with a raging toothache. After crossing the finish line, he had to find a dentist who removed the painful molar. On the stage to Metz, his rotten luck continued.

At Bazeilles, there was a mass crash, which happened just in front of the Sixth Moroccan Riflemen's Band which had carefully arranged itself at the edge of the road and, as the riders approached, they had started to play. They were lined up on the footpath amongst the crowds, some of whom were getting a little too carried away. As usual, the road was littered with cars and motorcycles. The press will go to any extreme to catch the best shot. Near the head of the peloton was a ciné cameraman who was perched on the spare wheel, mounted on the left hand side of his press car. His legs were astride the wheel, as if he was riding a horse. As the cars slowed, the drivers and the cameraman were distracted by the band and the encroaching crowd and the inevitable happened. There was the usual screeching of brakes and honking of horns and bikes being thrown in all directions. Vietto fell, and was the main victim. He went, head down, into the back of Pélissier and, under the impact, his glasses shattered. Miraculously, his eye was not severely injured but, when he got to his feet, his face covered in blood and his eyes were badly swollen. He had a deep cut above his eyebrow.

Such was the life of a cyclist in the Tour de France. Tragedy could strike at any minute and end a rider's race. Vietto would live to fight another day but, as if it was needed, each day brought a stark reminder, to Paco and his fellow sufferers, that their very existence in this race hung by a thread.

After the finish, the riders made their way to the Grand Hotel, where they lined up for a massage, showered and then tucked into their supper. The courtyard outside the hotel became a makeshift workshop. Half lit by the hotel lights, the mass of yellow bikes hung on their thin stands, their wheels in the air, waiting to be cleaned and prepared for the following day's stage. With the first major climb lying in wait for them, the riders were anxious to check that the correct gearing that they had selected had been fitted to their bikes.

From his hotel window, Paco could make out Maes, in his tracksuit and a pair of red slippers, in deep conversation with his mechanic. Pélissier was also there with his loyal mechanic, Paulo. He had ridden steadily today in preparation for Le Ballon d'Alsace. So confident was Pélissier of a good ride in the morning that he had opted for an eighteen tooth sprocket on his rear wheel.

Paco had asked for a twenty tooth sprocket and had already checked his machine. It was ten o'clock when he turned out his light. He could still hear the murmur of voices in the courtyard which would continue throughout the night. Breakfast was at two-thirty and he would be racing at four-thirty. His body was complaining, but he reminded himself that, often, when he felt the worst, he had performed his best. At this point, he was desperate for sleep and with that thought he closed his eyes and sank his weary head into the soft pillow.

Results of Stage 3

Winner: R. Di Paco, 4h. 29' 07"
F. Cepeda, 62nd, 4h. 37' 19"

Overall: R. Maes, 17h. 24' 34"
F. Cepeda, 80th, 18h. 30' 22"

12

THE ROAD GOES UP

July 7th, Stage 4, Metz to Belfort, 220kms, (31.411 kph)

I n the very early hours of the morning, an eagle-eyed milkman, making his deliveries on the outskirts of Metz, noticed a two kilometre stretch of road strewn with broke glass. Being a fan of the race, he knew the carnage that would be caused as a result of what seemed like a thoughtless and deliberate act. He immediately drove to the race headquarters and informed Henri Desgrange. The race route was diverted, to avoid this stretch, and the milkman was awarded a *L'Auto* medal for his actions.

The route between Metz and Belfort presented the riders with their first serious climb; the famous Ballon d'Alsace. This climb was a prologue to the more serious Alpine tests which would follow in the next few days. The Ballon d'Alsace would be an opportunity for the Italians, like Bertoni or Camusso, and other riders returning from the mountainous Tour of Italy, to show their climbing credentials. It was also an ideal opportunity for a new and unknown rider to announce himself.

Ordinarily, Paco might have fancied his chances but his legs were still inflamed and sore after the cobbled stages. He was also conscious that a double stage lay ahead, a seven hour first stage from Belfort to Geneva, followed by a fifty-eight kilometre time trial from Geneva to Evian. The previous day, Monsieur Desgrange had probably been wincing as the peloton moved through the Lorraine region at a pedestrian pace. The double stage was one of his innovations to shake up the race during the flat stages and ensure that the riders raced hard and earned their contracts. In previous Tours, Desgrange had threatened the riders with an individual time trial, if their average speed for a stage dropped below thirty kilometres per hour. Their welfare was never a high priority. The first time a double stage had been employed in the Tour was in 1934, when stage 21a, an eighty-one kilometre race from La Rochelle to La Roche-sur-Yon, was followed by the first ever individual time trial in the Tour. Shortly after arriving at the velodrome in La Roche-sur-Yon, the riders set off at two minutes intervals on the ninety kilometre second stage to Nantes. Some riders had less than ten minutes recovery before they started the individual time trial.

The riders had been wary of this double stage to Geneva since the route had been announced and there had been some talk of it already around the breakfast and supper tables. However, after three days of tough racing, the majority of the field was not thinking too far ahead. Paco was one of riders who was of this mindset. It was a case of taking one day at a time and focusing on what lay immediately ahead. Surviving the next stage, which included the first major climb of the Ballon d'Alsace, was his primary focus.

The riders left the start line in the Grand Place, in Metz, in beautiful sunshine and under a bluebird sky. It was a slow start for the first hour, more like a club run, and this allowed photographers to take some studied shots of the riders. The riders were in a lighthearted mood and chatted and laughed at each other's jokes.

They continued along the edge of the Moselle. The sweet smell of freshly cut hay gave way to the less pleasant smell of the engines of the following cars and motorcycles, as the Tour Caravan edged its way through the hollow of the valley. They passed small, white-washed houses, with red-tiled roofs, and climbed over hills of dense pine forests. They were closing in on the Ballon d'Alsace.

Amberg, who Paco knew from the Vuelta a España, was one of the favourites to take the honours and the prize money at the top of this climb. Earlier in the year, he had won the Mont Faron climb, one of Paco's favourite races. Amberg was a strong climber but he had little experience of riding in the Tour de France. He had been trained by the great Henri Pélissier, elder brother of Charles and the winner of the Tour in 1923. Pélissier had been suddenly killed by his lover, Camille Tharault, after a violent argument and struggle at the home they shared near Paris, two months before the start of the Tour. She had shot him five times with a revolver after he attacked her with a knife. Ironically, she used the same gun to kill Pélissier that Pélissier's first wife, Léonie, had used to take her own life in 1933. Amberg may have had thoughts of making a name for himself and dedicating the stage win to Pélissier, but he made the cardinal mistake of escaping too early. Making his move fifty kilometres before the start of the climb, Amberg burned all his matches before the main attack on the pass. Pushing a huge gear against an increasingly severe ramp, he was easily overhauled by the Belgians, Vervaecke, Jules Lowie and François Neuville. Vervaecke was no surprise, as he had been first to the top of this col the previous year, but the other two were newcomers and had made a big impact in their debut

Tour. The race had a way of unearthing these gems and Lowie and Neuville had surprised themselves as much as the crowds which lined the climb.

The Belgians dominated the day yet again. After crossing the pass, Lowie faded but a small group formed, including the German, Oskar Thierbach, and the four Belgians, Aerts, Danneels, the current Belgian champion, Vervaecke and Neuville. The sprinter Aerts went on to win the stage, on a beautiful Sunday afternoon, in the velodrome of Champ de Mars. Raising his right arm in victory, he acknowledged the cheers of the banked masses. It was Belgium's second victory since leaving Paris.

It was a tough day for the rest of the field, strung out by the time they reached the foot of the climb and already having lost the opportunity of a good ranking on the stage. Archambaud was having his usual bad luck, puncturing three times, while Speicher punctured twice and had a fall that could have been quite serious. The race leader, Maes, was over two minutes down before the climb, but he did not panic and climbed impressively. He then pushed hard on the flat and only finished ten seconds behind the winner, holding on to his yellow jersey. His strong finish sent an ominous warning to the French team, who had perhaps hoped that, when faced with the climbs, he would wilt and pay for his early heroics. However, Maes had confounded his critics and had stood up to the first challenge.

Paco climbed the Ballon steadily in the company of the Germans, Georg Stach and Kurt Stöepel. Pélissier was with them for a while but he soon slipped back. He usually did when the road went upwards. Again there were punctures galore, reminding everyone, if they needed reminding, that fate played a huge part in this brutal race. Paco hardly saw his compatriots throughout the day and four of the Spanish team finished behind him, raising questions about their commitment to this Tour. This was particularly true of Vicente Trueba, who finished twenty-four minutes down on the leader and fifteen minutes behind Paco. Paco felt that, for the first time on the Tour, he had justified his place in the race. Finishing the day racing in the company of Archambaud and the impressive Germans and ahead of Pélissier gave him great encouragement.

Results of Stage 4

Winner: J. Aerts, 7h. 00' 14"
F. Cepeda, 56th, 7h. 09'04"

Overall: R. Maes, 24h. 24' 58"
F. Cepeda, 76th, 25h. 39' 20"

13

DREADED DOUBLE STAGE

July 8th, Stage 5a, Belfort to Geneva, 262 kms, (31.354 kph)

The stage from Belfort to Geneva would be an absolute brute. It began at four-thirty, in the gloom of the morning, in frozen mists, outside the Brassiere Danjean, a popular restaurant and cafe. The riders had risen at two-thirty and come down to breakfast at three. Most seemed in a daze and not much was eaten compared to normal race days. Paco forced himself to eat his normal breakfast but noticed that his Spanish teammates were unusually quiet. Perhaps Vicente Trueba, the team captain, was licking his wounds after his poor showing the previous day. Something was wrong, as Trueba was usually the last of the Spaniards to leave the breakfast table. This morning he ate very little and left without even speaking to Paco.

Despite the ungodly hour, a huge crowd still gathered for the only night start to a stage. Men and women stood six or seven deep on both sides of the street to watch the grand depart. The riders were tightly packed, with their fresh white caps illuminated in the gloom. Monsieur Cazalis signalled the start of the stage by flashing his torch. Slowly the riders rolled away, into the mist, on what would be a monstrous day, split into two stages.

The first stage took them from Belfort to Geneva, covering two hundred and eighty-two kilometres and then, after a short rest, in the late afternoon, in what became an oppressive heat, they would embark on a time trial of fifty-eight kilometres, from Geneva to Evian.

By the time the riders crossed the River Doubs for the first time, at the Pont-de Roide, in Vermondans, it was still cool but at least it was now daylight. Magne led Archambaud and then, twelve kilometres later, the Doubs was crossed again, at Saint-Hippolyte, with another Frenchman, Debenne, at the head. It looked like the French team had planned to control the race and wrestle the initiative away from the Belgians. The route followed the river, which wound its way through a steep, meandering valley. The views were constantly changing but the riders were focussed on the task which lay ahead, as they headed towards the first slopes of the Jura mountains. The French were still setting the pace, as they led the peloton over the first few inclines.

The countryside was green and there was plenty of shade from the trees to give the riders some protection against the intensity of the sun. The pine trees which populated the higher hills had still not come into view, as Antonin Magne led the peloton though the rolling landscape and the peaceful gorges of the Doubs. For a moment, as the peloton rolled on, Paco took a moment to savour this scene; the undulating countryside, a herd of cows grazing on a small isle in the middle of the river, a bell tower and a train puffing out its plume of smoke on the hillside.

For the most part, it would be a slow, monotonous procession. The Sabine Pass was a serious climb and was followed by the Faucille which was less severe. Both were climbed without too much pain. Only, Paul Chocque, whose legs were pumping like pistons, provoked the anger of the other riders, for pushing the peloton along too quickly. There was of course the usual spectacle of the feed station. At Champignole, large crowds had gathered. They had amassed themselves behind the tables and were laughing and cheering at the chaos. One or two excited fans had edged their way into the road, hoping one of the riders might ask them to hold a bicycle whilst they rifled the table for nourishment. Caps, hats, boaters, berets and paper hats, handed out by sponsors, made this a colourful scene. Some of the young boys and young men had even groomed their hair in the style of their favourite riders. Some riders made an immediate assault on the tables, grabbing whatever food they could lay their hands on; others seemed less impatient and waited their turn.

By the end of the day, the sun was baking hot on the dusty slopes of the Jura, where the golden rays flooded the gorges of the Lemme. The photographers and the ciné cameramen loved the mountains. It was here that they could take their most dramatic shots. But those beautiful landscapes were the curse of the bad climbers and the sprinters. The riders would now be constantly battling fierce gradients, with the exception of the Marseille to Perpignan stage, until the twenty-second of July, when the race arrived in Pau. For now, most of the main field rolled along in peace but they knew, and many feared, what was coming.

By now, it was becoming clear that the race was developing into a battle between two men, Antonin Magne and Romain Maes, and the other riders watched them as they watched each other. Magne, or Tonin to his teammates and French fans, followed Maes's shadow for the majority of the stage. On the road up to the Col de la Savine, the riders were strung out in a line like ants on the march. They conserved their energy knowing that, the second stage, the dreaded race against the clock, was still to come.

As the peloton climbed the Col de la Faucille, lush vegetation turned to more barren, rocky slopes. Rocks protruded from between the exposed pines and only the odd pasture remained. But the group stayed intact and seemed to ride at a leisurely pace. On the lower, gradual slopes, there were few spectators. Paco was conscious of small groups of men standing on walls or on banks adjacent to the road. The more sensible ones took to the shade of the tall pines but some stood out in the blazing heat of the sun, their jackets discarded and their white shirtsleeves rolled up.

As the riders crested the summit, at one thousand, three hundred and thirty metres, the crowds increased. The cars of some spectators, the ones who had arrived early, with their picnics and, of course, large amounts of wine and beer, and some of the official cars of the newsmen and photographers, were perched on the outer edge of the road or parked in rows among the rocks on the bend. It was a typical scene from the Tour de France; a policeman patrolling the road, women in berets and casual dress, men in shirtsleeves, film cameramen and photographers standing on roofs of cars or on the back seats of convertibles, a journalist sitting on the roof of his car taking notes and recording the times. They were all mesmerised by this dramatic show, each one trying to find a unique shot of their favourite rider. And beyond this human wall, there was nothing but the void of the precipice and the shimmering haze of the Jura heat.

It seemed unlikely that the group would finish together, as they began their descent towards the banks of Lake Léman and Geneva, on the French-Swiss border. Sure enough, it was a Frenchman, Archambaud, who attacked. Up to this point, he had been keeping his powder dry, lurking in the middle of the group, but he made a breakaway and had better luck than he did in the Charleville to Metz stage. He managed to enter Geneva's velodrome alone, a few seconds ahead of the Belgian De Caluwé, who was, in turn, followed by his countryman, Danneels. It was a quiet and calm crowd that welcomed Archambaud, as he completed his lap of the velodrome. Even though both sides of the track were filled with spectators and officials, as well as the main stand, only one or two hands waved in appreciation. Perhaps it was the oppressive heat that had dampened their spirits.

The other riders crossed the line shortly afterwards, in dribs and drabs, including Paco, who finished forty-second, his best placing so far. However, he had little time to celebrate. His main concern, along with his fellow riders, was to find something to eat and drink and then some shade, from the merciless heat, behind the main stand where some tents had been erected. Some spectators, out of sympathy for the suffering of the riders, had thrown fruit to them. Peaches and apricots rained down. Suddenly, Paco spotted a tasty peach lying in the dust. He picked it up, wiped it and then devoured it. Its juices dribbled down his chin.

Spechier spotted him on all fours, crawling around in search of more peaches and saw his opportunity to play the joker, at Paco's expense. It was the oldest French joke in the book but he could not resist it. Seeing Paco scouring the parched earth for another piece of fruit, he shouted at him, at the top of his voice, as if Paco was deaf.

'Tu vas à la pêche?' ('Are you going fishing?')

Paco did not really understand fully what he had said, so he ignored him and carried on scanning the ground for another peach.

Spechier shouted again, even louder this time. 'Alors, vous allez à la pêche!' ('So you are going fishing!')

Paco looked up, seemingly confused, and shouted back,

equally as loudly, in his simple French, 'Non! je vais à la pêche!'
('No! I am going fishing!')

Speicher burst into howls of laughter, shook his head and
walked off. Paco was left mystified. Paco had thought he had
replied, 'I'm getting a peach.' He had not realised that he
had inadvertently delivered the punch line to Speicher's silly
joke.

The riders needed to rehydrate and rest their tired limbs in
preparation for the second great challenge of the day. Some
poured buckets of cold water over their heads to cool themselves after they crossed the finish line. Paco made his way
straight to the showers, underneath the main stand, where
some of the riders sat stripped to their waists. They resembled
miners coming up from the bowels of the earth. Their faces
were tired and grubby, their torsos lily white in comparison to
their bronzed arms and necks. The heat had been almost intolerable but Paco had survived better than some. He caught sight
of his friend, poor Figueras, who was now in the lantern rouge
position. Paco saw him pushing his bike towards the showers,
limping badly. His arm and shoulder were covered with
bandages, as were his right wrist and left knee. His jersey was
torn and he looked a sorry fellow. It was his first Tour de
France. What a baptism!

The stage, in short, would have been undramatic if it had
not been marked by a bunch of abandonments. Three
touristes-routiers, Pierre Janvier, Paul-René Coralini, and
Sezny Leroux, plus the Spanish trio of Aces, Trueba, Ezquerra
and Cañardo, had left the race. The loss of three of the
Spanish national team decimated the squad. It was completely
unexpected and bewildering. It was especially shocking that,
Trueba, the specialist climber, who had inspired his team on so
many occasions, should quit on the eve of the big mountains.
Rumours were rife, as was normal in the peloton. There was a
bad spirit amongst the Spanish riders, some said. Others

asserted that it was simply a question of money. They weren't earning enough.

No more than thirty kilometres into the stage, in the fairly steep hills, beyond Saint-Hippolyte, Trueba, Ezquerra, Canardo and the French touriste-routier, Janvier, had been spotted riding at the speed of a funeral procession. They were dragging themselves miserably along the road. They were already an hour outside the race schedule set by the organisers. Was it lack of preparation on the part of the riders? Mr Huerta, from *Noti-Sport*, in Madrid, offered an explanation and an insight into the mindset of Trueba, at the start of the Tour.

'Vicente Trueba did not want to ride the Tour,' said Huerta. 'He came because his younger brother was sick and he did not want the Tour organisation to accuse the Trueba family of boycotting a race to which they owed so much. He left Spain reluctantly because he would rather have stayed at home with his young wife and attended to his business interests. He had just bought a new garage.'

It is most likely that Trueba had lost his motivation. The money he had earned from cycling, thanks to the Tour de France, had been more than enough to make ends meet. Believing his brother Firmín would be riding the Tour, until he became ill, Vicente did not take enough care with his own preparations and, after three hard stages, he did not have the will to continue. That is what the Spanish press and the Tour organisation blamed him for. Spain was an emerging cycling nation and the press was eager for success. There was increasing pressure on the Spanish riders to challenge the French, the Belgians and the Italians. What was most regrettable about this situation was that Trueba persuaded Ezquerra and Cañardo to join him. Ezquerra, that very morning, in Belfort, had told reporters of his joy in riding the Tour and how he was eagerly anticipating the arrival of the Alps. He was certainly not talking about giving up. However, Ezquerra was young and it seemed that he had allowed himself to be persuaded otherwise.

Whatever their reason or reasons for leaving, everyone took a dim view of it. None of the Spanish riders appeared injured and their sudden decision to abandon the Tour de France lacked class. Trueba and Ezquerra, in particular, would surely have featured prominently in the Alps which lay around the corner.

Paco had ridden with and against Trueba for many years and he was dumbfounded when he first heard rumours that the three Spaniards would not be starting the time-trial. If it were true, then he needed to talk to them. He was sure that he would be able to make them see sense. But they were nowhere to be found and it was stifling hot out in the sun. Paco needed to find some shade in one of the tents and rest before the second stage of the day began.

Results of Stage 5a

Winner: M. Archambaud, 8h. 21' 22"
F. Cepeda, 42nd, 8h. 26' 20"

Overall: R. Maes, 32h. 47' 51"
F. Cepeda, 71st, 33h. 05' 40"

14

RACE AGAINST THE CLOCK

July 8th, Geneva to Evian, Individual Time-Trial, 58kms,
(35.728 kph)

For some journalists, the large number of abandonments made great news. It was an opportunity for those who were no great friends of Desgrange to have a dig at him. These split stages, they thought, were an attempt by Desgrange to revitalise the interest in the Tour in the days leading up to the mountains; an innovation to prevent the riders from becoming complacent and taking it easy before the gradients began to bite. This was an opportunity for the left wing press and communist newspapers to heap scorn upon Desgrange, for exploiting the riders for his own ends. The Tour was seen as a Capitalist venture, a business project, from which industrialists profited and riders were labourers to be exploited. The riders grumbled about the split stages but they had no choice. They looked upon themselves as companions of misfortune.

Paco was no stranger to the time trial. On the contrary, in Spain, he had excelled against the clock. However, no one was accustomed to riding a time trial of almost sixty kilometres, having already spent more than eight gruelling hours in the saddle. This put the second demi-stage into a hellish category. The Tour was painful enough, without this new addition.

The time trial presents riders with a special challenge. When riding in a peloton, a rider can feed off the presence of other riders on the road. He feels the excitement of riding in a bunch and the others help to drive him on, so that even his rivals can be a support. On the road, riding in the peloton there is company. It is a brotherhood which acts as a distraction to the rider. It helps make the long hours pass, the kilometres seem to tick by more quickly, and thoughts of abandonment are diminished, when the going gets tough. However, in the time trial, when a rider is alone on the road, those worries are more difficult to banish and it is then that cruel and insidious thoughts play on the mind. In some ways, it was harder for riders like Paco to cast aside these doubts, knowing that they had no chance in the general classification. For the Aces, there was always the lure of the yellow jersey, the possibility of a stage win, or finishing on the podium in Paris to spur them on. Paco's main aim was still to arrive in Paris in one piece and to climb well in the mountain stages which would dominate the race in the following days. The hills and the mountains were his domain, where he felt most at home. A mountain stage win would be the crowning glory of his career.

Paco's start number in the time trial was forty-seven and he had Di Paco starting one minute behind him. He began his time trial with an air of resignation. It was a case of surviving the race against the clock rather than racing against the clock. There was a large crowd at the start to see each rider leave Geneva but as Paco left the city, and wound his way towards Evian, the crowds diminished. He was tired and, for the first few kilometres, he felt like he was having to force his battered and weary legs to push against the pedals. It did not help that Di Paco flew past him after about five kilometres. Forget him, thought Paco. In a couple of days, when we hit the mountains, he won't look so good. Paco continued to roll along and, as the Italian disappeared from view, the stiffness gradually began to ease from his legs and he settled into a better rhythm.

If the rumours were true about the abandonment of his three Spanish teammates, it made Paco all the more proud of his own strength and determination to carry on and finish in the Parc des Princes, in Paris. Like them, he had had contemplated abandonment on that first night, after he had trailed home at the back of the field. Then, on the terrible pave of the North, his knees had swelled like footballs with the pounding and the shaking. Along with practically every other rider, he had been dreading this double stage. Nor did he have the protection and the camaraderie generated by being in a team. He was riding alone and had to make alliances with others wherever he could. Yet, he had carried on when it would have been easier to throw in the towel. He was pretty sure that this would be his last Tour de France and he was not about to give up without a fight. He had suffered unbearably in his previous Tours and had pushed himself to his uttermost limits. Paco was hurting, but he was not at the point of giving up yet.

Paco rolled into Evian in forty-seventh position, some eleven minutes behind Di Paco who had gone on to win the stage. He now had a rest day to look forward to, and he hoped his body and mind might heal over the next twenty-four hours.

After the time trial, rumours began circulating almost immediately. Di Paco was at the centre of them. How did he manage to be four minutes down on Archambaud and two minutes down on Magne at the half way point, but then finish in Evian a few seconds ahead of them both? It would be impossible to follow each rider with an official car but, with so many long, deserted stretches between villages, for an experienced rider, it was not beyond his capability to mobilise some vehicles behind which he could draft. Magne was also being talked about. Some suggested he had been given assistance by some of his teammates and turned the individual time trial into a team time trial. The results certainly suggested this might have happened.

At least one competitor was caught, riding behind a motorcycle with a wire clenched between his teeth, a throwback to some of the daft antics of the pre-war years. Several riders were under suspicion and the commissioners held a meeting to try to decide the most difficult cases. Following their review, multiple sanctions were handed out. Pélissier, Debenne and René Bernard were penalised by two minutes and fined two hundred francs, and Fayolle and Prior by one minute, with a twenty-five francs fine. Di Paco was fined one hundred francs, while Magne escaped with a warning for having taken advantage of forming a pack. Bernard found himself demoted from third to sixth place overall. There were grumbles the penalties had been too lenient on the French riders and there were feelings there had been some favouritism towards the home team but, naturally, no one confronted Desgrange. No one talked aloud and Paco did not care to think too much about such things. It was all he could do to drag himself to his bed that evening. He loved this race but there was no escaping its brutality.

At supper that evening, the news that Trueba, Ezquerra and Cañardo had abandoned became official. They had headed back to Spain, on the eve of the great mountains. They could have at least waited a few more days, Paco thought. He was looking forward to the mountains where he would be more at home, but the knowledge that three of his countryman would not be with him left him with a heavy heart. He felt sure that, had he been given the chance to speak to them, he could have persuaded them to continue, but they had departed too quickly and suddenly. Paco was now the leading Spanish climber in the race so there would be added pressure on him to perform well in the mountains. To some extent he would be shouldering the hopes and dreams of the Spanish racing fans, as well as his own.

Results of Stage 5b

Winner: R. Di Paco, 1h. 37' 24"
F. Cepeda, 47th, 1h. 48'31"

Overall: R. Maes, 34h. 25' 55"
F. Cepeda, 64th, 35h. 54' 44"

15

REST AND RECUPERATION

July 9th, Evian, Rest Day

The waters of Lake Geneva lapped gently against the shore and the sun's rays danced on the water as the riders enjoyed a well-earned rest in the spa resort of Evian. The rest day was a day for reading newspapers or taking strolls along the lake side, drinking coffee in cafes, posing with fans and signing autographs. The more energetic might take a boat onto the lake. Towards the end of the afternoon, the riders retired to their rooms, where reporters were finally given the opportunity to approach them to chat a little about their Tour experiences.

Unsurprisingly, the Belgians gave the impression of calm, quiet strength and great optimism. Romain Maes, holder of yellow jersey since the first stage from Paris, appeared fresh, unscathed, and without the slightest trouble. Worryingly for the French fans, who had hoped, by this stage, he would begin to show some cracks, his morale was excellent.

It was unusual for the leader of the race to be showing such confidence ahead of the most difficult stages, but Maes seemed cheerful and confident. No doubt, deep down, he must have been a little worried by what awaited him in the mountains. He could not have forgotten that, the previous year, he had not even figured among the best climbers. But the young Belgian was now beginning to seriously worry his rivals. Wearing the yellow jersey, with the promise of winning the famous trophy, can undoubtedly give a rider unimaginable sources of energy and renewed strength.

The journalists' copy filled columns discussing whether or not Maes would be able to succeed and hold onto his position through the challenging cols of the Alps. Both the French press, which was unashamedly biased, and the French riders, thought not and hoped not. They were of the opinion that he had surpassed himself, compared to his previous moderate performances. In the Alps, it was not simply a case of two or three passes. After the Aravis and the Galibier, then there were the passes of Laffrey, Vars, Allos, Castillon, Braus, and Sospel. The French were unanimous in thinking that, after pushing himself to his limits establishing a lead, the Belgian would eventually be forced to surrender his treasured yellow jersey.

The French did their best to ignore the confidence radiating from the Belgian camp. Yet practically everyone else in the peloton, including Paco, had to admit the Belgian team was stronger than in previous years. Not only did the men seem happier they also seemed to have a much better team spirit. So far, they had not had any of the arguments which, in previous campaigns, had disrupted the harmony of the team. This time, the group had an impressive bond which probably came from the fact that, since leaving Paris, they had been in complete control of the race, both as a team and individually. Since the creation of the national teams, the prize money flowed into a common fund, and that went a long way to motivate a team to work together.

The Belgian champion, Danneels, who was making his debut in the Tour, had also made quite an impression. His performances on the Ballon d'Alsace suggested he would climb well in the cols and that he could finish high up in the overall rankings, by the time the race arrived in Paris. The powerful Edgard De Caluwé had also given great support to his leader since Paris. Vervaecke was another who had shown what he could do on the Ballon d'Alsace. Being a good climber, he could also be one to watch in the mountains.

The Italians, who were usually, for the French, the most formidable opponents, had so far offered no threat. They seemed low on morale and ideas and, although Bergamaschi was pretty well placed in the overall standings, he could not really be considered a challenger. Paco rated Camusso and Bertoni from the Italian team. They could be in contention in the Alpine passes but, so far, their ambition seemed to be limited to fulfilling their contracts.

The Germans were disciplined to a man. They were mostly debutants, but had been impressive, calm and tenacious. These youngsters were athletic, powerful and, despite their inexperience, were acquitting themselves well, even though their leader, Stöpel, was not on form because he had been suffering from saddle boils.

Much to Paco's disappointment and frustration, the Spanish team had not shown much application and unity. Now, with only Prior, Alvarez, Cardona, and Elys, from the official Spanish national squad, still riding, the Spanish could no longer be considered a threat. Paco was appalled at the actions of Trueba, Ezquerra and Canardo, suddenly giving up without a valid reason. This was a unique situation for the Tour de France and dealt a mortal blow to the Spanish Association.

Wearing the Spanish colours, in the past, had filled Paco with pride and he could not comprehend the actions of the three.

The early stages over the cobbles had been fast and painful, and the numerous crashes, the unpredictable new metal rims and the punctures had eroded the riders' confidence. And then the demi-stage, in the oppressive heat, had required the riders to plumb the depths of their mental and physical resources. But this was the Tour de France and every rider who signed up for it knew that the race would impose the most appalling physical and psychological demands upon them. Other than those in the top ten of the overall standings, thoughts of abandonment must have plagued the minds of most of the field, on more than one occasion. Paco himself had harboured these thoughts but learnt to banish them quickly. His fellow countrymen had given into their demons and they would have to live with that knowledge.

Paco knew that he would now be offered a place on the Spanish national team, as the rules allowed for an individual rider to be promoted to his national team in the event of that team becoming depleted. However, he had no intention of accepting the offer. He had not been worthy of a place in the team when the Spanish national squad was selected and he felt nothing had changed on that score. He would rather the opportunity for promotion had never occurred. There had been little expectation on the shoulders of the Spanish riders and, yet, three of them had ended up in the broom wagon.

In contrast, the weight of expectation on the French team was enough to sink a battleship, especially with the emergence of this strong young Belgian squad. Nevertheless, Magne, remained stoic and measured and spoke to the press with his usual frankness, when interviewed.

'I think that I still have a good chance of winning the Tour. Yesterday, in the stage against the clock, I made a small blunder, because I committed the error of not having anything to eat from Geneva. But that is nothing; in the mountains, I will be at my business. I have made the least amount of effort from Paris. Unless there are unforeseen circumstances, I think I'll wear the yellow jersey before the end of the Alps. Will I keep it to the end? That is another story.'

Speicher was also full of confidence. 'I feel as good as I did two years ago and I think I will climb better than usual, taking advantage of my experience from the previous Tour de France.'

Even Vietto, despite being thirty-five minutes adrift, and with the multiple roles he had played since leaving Paris, still held the hope that he might wear the precious yellow jersey.

'I am climbing in much the same way as I was last year. I have not lost the Tour de France yet, believe me. Last year, in Evian, I was further behind than I am this year, and yet I almost won. Trueba and Ezquerra are no longer there, so I will be much less worried at the top of the cols and so I will also benefit from larger bonuses. And then there are the famous stages of the four Pyrenean passes; if I really climb like before then what is a thirty-five minute deficit? On previous occasions Ottavio Bottecchia and Lucien Buysse have won stages there an hour in front of the field. This year, I will make some modifications to my tactics and my gears. But wait and see. I'm not going to give anything away.'

This positive spirit was shared amongst Paco's rival individual riders and was, in some cases, sharper than amongst some of the riders from the national teams. The Belgians, Antoon Dignef, Lowie and Neuville were performing well and the Germans, Ickes, Bruno Roth and Georges Haendel could easily have merited a place in their national teams, but it was the Frenchman, Pélissier, who was the outstanding individual performer and he was more popular than ever with the crowds and the media.

'This is the first time that I have done a Tour de France so easily and so quietly,' he said. 'Look, I do not have a single scratch, I sleep like an angel and I have no one to look after. Long live the category of Individuals!'

Paco could not claim to be as confident as Pélissier. He was overconfident, Paco thought, and could do with a little more humility. You never knew what lay in wait around the next corner and there had been so many accidents already. Paco would never dare tempt fate in the way that Pélissier had done. But Pélissier knew how to play to the crowd, even though his comments and his showmanship did not always sit comfortably with his fellow riders.

The twenty-ninth Tour de France divided itself naturally into five parts, determined by the design of the route. It started with the five flat stages between Paris and Evian, bringing the riders to the foothills of the mountains. From there, they would battle over the brutish Alpine cols for a further five days. There would be a brief lull in the toil as they journeyed between Cannes and Perpignan, but the assault against the mountains would begin again in the rugged Pyrenees. Finally, after leaving Pau, on the fifteenth stage, the riders would begin the long road back to Paris.

Now in Evian, on a much-needed rest day, having survived part one, it was time for a brief period of rest. None of the riders had arrived at the foot of the Alps fresh, despite Pélissier's comment. The initial stages had revealed the state of each rider's preparation, and Paco was honest enough to admit that his preparations had been inadequate. But he was far from being alone in that respect. Even some of the favourites had not been on top form, relying on those early flat stages to properly break themselves in. Those testing flat stages of the north were no less important than the Alpine stages. They may have carried less prestige than the mountain stages, but, already, some of the top riders, who had left Paris with a chance of winning, were now out of contention. They would have to content themselves with an honourable finish. As in previous years, this year's race would probably come down to a battle between two or three of the stars from the Aces.

The formation of the national teams had not improved this situation. In the past, riders who were sponsored by the manufacturers had ridden for their designated team leader and now the situation was the same; the national teams were riding for their main man, their captain. Those riders who had lost a lot of time at the beginning of the race were no longer interested in defending their general classification positions. Their only thoughts were to defend their leader and make as much money as possible for the team. By finishing the race in Paris, they would be entitled to a share of the prize money awarded to the entire team.

For individual riders, like Paco, or the touristes-routiers, who were not competing for the top spot, their only hope was to win a stage or more realistically be the first rider to reach a mountain col. The majority of riders were now simply working for their leader, which might mean they end up finishing sixty-fifth at the top of the Galibier instead of tenth. So, while some of the riders were focused on conscientiously doing their job, others, like Paco, were fighting only for themselves and might find an opportunity to taste some glory as a result.

Paco had gone for a short stroll along the promenade and chatted with some riders over a coffee but he was in pain and wanted some time to himself. That evening he had no desire to write in his diary but he felt an obligation to write a quick letter to Mr Monchin at the offices of *El Pueblo Vasco*. Paco knew his fans would be eager to know his latest thoughts on the race and particularly his views on the abandonment of the Spanish riders but both his body and his mind were exhausted. Nevertheless he took up his pen.

Evian, July 9th, Rest Day.

Mr. Monchin – Bilbao

Dear Sir,

I am very sorry to tell you that because I am suffering a muscle strain in my left knee that needs much rest, today, being a rest day, I cannot send some lines to the readers of El Pueblo Vasco.

I just take this opportunity to send everybody my warmest greetings from this beautiful town of Evian, and declare that, regardless of the 'disaster' that has happened, and which has provoked huge discouragement, I ride on with the same excitement as before. Providing that God gives me health, I will arrive in Paris, whatever my position.

Again, I send my greetings. Francisco Cepeda

16

INTO THE ALPS

July 10th, Stage 6, Evian to Aix-Les-Bains, 207 kilometres,
(32.369 kph)

F ollowing the rest day, there was an air of expectation
as the riders gathered for the dropping of the flag and
the first proper Alpine stage of the Tour. Tension was
etched on their faces, and those of their followers.

The road from Evian to Aix-les-Bains would pass through
the Aravis Pass and the Tamié Pass, the latter less famous, but
more formidable, than the former. The leading positions were
still up for grabs. It was true that Maes had dominated up to
now, but the winner the previous year, Magne, Bergamaschi
and even Speicher were beginning to look menacing. Vietto
had not yet figured, but he was sure to make a move in the
mountains.

Between Evian and the Aravis, nothing much happened.
The peloton was ambling along slowly, rolling lazily towards
Thonon. The journalist, Jean Antoine, realising that the

Spanish abandonments opened the door for some of the Spanish individuals to be promoted to the national team and wear the purple, yellow and red jersey, drove alongside the director's car. Through the window he asked Manchon, Henri Desgrange's travelling companion, which riders would be promoted from the Spanish individuals.

'No one,' came the blunt reply.

'But why?'

'Demetrio, Cepeda and Bâchero have not even asked. They consider themselves unworthy of the title of Ace. I think they are wrong but there it is. You have your answer.'

Indeed, Paco would have more than merited such a promotion, but his response demonstrated the humility for which he was well known and well respected.

As he pedalled along in the main bunch, Paco was thinking that if Trueba, Ezquerra and Cañardo had not withdrawn from the race, then Spain might have had a chance of victory on this stage. Once he was back on his bike and had ridden a few kilometres, the soreness and pain from his knees had gradually diminished and, in many ways, he was feeling stronger and more positive than ever. Although he had not come to Paris in peak condition, he had hoped that, day by day, he would improve in strength and stamina and this seemed to be the case. Had Trueba still been in the race, Paco might have been able to help him, in spite of his status as an individual, but alas, Trueba was gone and there was no point in dwelling on that thought. The three Spanish Aces were, no doubt, at this minute, on their way home, sitting in a comfortable railway carriage. Paco quickly banished the image, as the riders were heading towards the beautiful resort of La Clusaz, eighty-five kilometres into the stage. There they would encounter the first Alpine col of the 1935 Tour de France.

The peloton was now riding at a very good tempo but no-one really knew where the first attack would come from. The

Belgians saw no advantage in stirring things up because their leader, Romain Maes, did not have a great background as a climber. Magne remained his most serious opponent but the Aravis was not a testing enough climb on which to launch an attack, if he wanted to gain any distance and time on a rider like Maes. As they left La Clusaz, there were a few skirmishes at the head of the peloton, set off first by Archambaud and then Bertoni, Vervaecke and Morelli. Maes and the field responded and they remained locked together as the road stretched out towards the col.

But suddenly, a blue silhouette appeared on the dusty road ahead, bordered on each side by green slopes, where cows grazed on the fresh mountain pastures, oblivious to the drama unfolding around them. As the climb steepened towards the col, the road began to zig zag. It also narrowed, as it was lined with hundreds of spectators and a long line of parked cars. This was a favourite spot for spectators, as the Aravis pass was easily accessible from Geneva and Evian. It was also an ideal spot from which to launch an attack which the classy Vietto knew and had planned. As he went clear, the crowds were waving and cheering in delight. Last year's sensation had regained his form and was flying up the mountain. Behind him the field was blown to pieces.

Paco sensed the confusion spreading around him. Several riders dropped back immediately when the pace started to increase. And now there was a faller. Paco thought it was the Italian, Eugenio Gestri but he did not have time to look back. He was weaving in and out of riders who were already struggling to push their pedals against the big gears. Most of the riders had not yet changed their wheels in favour of lower gears. Their legs were already heaving against the gradient and this was nowhere near the worst of the climbs. Di Paco was going backwards. Merviel and Debenne were also struggling, along with most of the young Germans. How quickly fortunes changed in the Tour.

Meanwhile, Vietto was over the summit of the col and descended well, perhaps even better than he had climbed, holding off Sylvère Maes and Alvarez. Neuville and Archambaud crossed the col together, ahead of Amberg and Gianello, and then the peloton of stars, including Romain Maes, Magne, Le Grevès, Bergamaschi, Morelli, Lowie, Gabriel Ruozzi, and Georg Umbenhauer, crossed.

After the speedy descent, there were about twenty kilometres of flat, before the riders arrived at the Tamié pass. This was a tougher proposition. Vietto approached the neck of the Tamié and, having changed his wheel after Aravis, gave the impression that he was climbing with even more ease. At the top, he was two minutes and ten seconds ahead of Sylvère Maes and two minutes and fifty-five seconds clear of Maes, Magne, Archambaud, Morelli and Neuville. Camusso was having a very difficult day and was over six minutes in arrears and, further adrift, Louis Hardiquest and Leducq, threw insults at the reporters.

'Ah! 'Bollocks! Bollocks!'

Without flinching, Vietto flew down the rough descent of the Tamié and rode alone along the spectacular road towards Annecy, skirting the famous lake. The clear waters shone like a mirror. Bravely, he continued his effort, although there was still more than thirty-five kilometres to ride before the finish in Aix-les-Bains.

In Annecy, the chasers closed the gap. Vietto's lead was reduced to one minute and fifty-five seconds on the peloton. He probably should have been caught, but the pack, which had suddenly grown through successive attacks, and was now swelled by the presence of Speicher, Le Grevès, Bergamaschi and Camusso, eased up and took a breather. This enabled

Vietto, who had not significantly slowed, to establish his winning margin.

In Annecy, he was almost two minutes in advance of the main field. In Saint-Félix, fifteen kilometres away, his lead had increased to two minutes and forty seconds and finally, in Aix-les-Bains, he crossed the finish line with a margin of four minutes and ten seconds on the peloton. In the sprint for second place, Le Grevès was the strongest, in front of Bergamaschi, Ambrogio Morelli and Romain Maes.

The enigmatic Vietto was the great hero of the day. Breaking away towards the top of the Aravis, he had climbed with ease and, having battled alone to maintain his lead for one hundred and twenty-five kilometres, he arrived in Aix-les-Bains a worthy and popular winner.

It was an impressive performance that won the admiration of everyone. Vietto's form had suddenly returned; the king of the mountains of the Tour de France, in 1934, was back in business.

Vietto had started the day in twenty-sixth place, over thirty minutes behind the yellow jersey but, with time bonuses added to his winning margin, he was able to reduce his deficit by seven minutes and twenty-four seconds. He had climbed to sixteenth in the general classification and the feeling was the man from Cannes was on the march up the overall standings. The previous year, he had made a similar move in the Alps, reducing his deficit, between Cannes and Aix-les-Bains, by twenty-four minutes on the leader. He might have even challenged Magne that year had it not been for the famous sacrifice he was forced to make in the Pyrenees, which would find a place in Tour de France folklore.

When Vietto had crossed the Col de Puymorens in the lead, he was forced, a little after l'Hospitalet, to give up his front wheel to his leader, Antonin Magne, after Magne had fallen off on a bend and buckled his front wheel. As a loyal domestique, Vietto had to sit on the roadside and wait for the service truck to give him a new wheel. Vietto discovered how to lose well that day. He became a national hero and the picture of him sitting by the side of the road, with his head in his hands, in tears, won the hearts of the nation. The following day, on the stage from Aix-les-Thermes to Luchon, he once again led over the Col de Portet d'Aspet but, on hearing that Magne had broken his chain, Vietto turned around and cycled five hundred metres back down the mountain to find his leader to give up his bike. His loyalty enabled Magne to go on and win the Tour.

The twenty-year-old had already won three stages that year and was on his way to winning the King of the Mountains competition. Many people thought he could have won the Tour in 1934, had it not been for the sacrifices he made for Magne. Whether that was true or not will never be known, but the young rider's sacrifices certainly made him famous and popular with the crowds. He earned much more money than Magne, as he became the main attraction at the post-Tour criteriums. The French fans loved him and named him King René.

Could Vietto still win the Tour this year? With the bulk of the Alps and Pyrenees still to come, his deficit of almost twenty-nine minutes, at Aix-les-Bains, was not looking so bad in comparison to his position in 1934.

Once again, Maes, whose climbing, the previous year, had appeared mediocre, defended his yellow jersey with an impressive heart and will. He stuck like glue to the wheel of Magne, who did not appear particularly strong and showed no desire to test his rival. The broad-shouldered Maes, hunched over his machine, chin slightly raised, elbows splayed, seemed completely focused on his task. Most of his teammates were dropped on the flat road after the Tamié pass, about ten kilometres from Annecy.

Behind Vietto, there was the isolated figure of Sylvère Maes, then a small group, including Romain Maes, Magne, Archambaud, Morelli and Neuville. Maes was a leader with no one to lead and, no doubt, was feeling a little exposed. Someone from the Caravan, presumably with Belgian sympathies, must have told Sylvère Maes that it might be a good idea for him to ease up in order to help defend his captain's yellow jersey.

It proved to be an inspirational moment. Incredibly, as the group was catching up with Sylvère Maes, who had sat up and was soft pedalling, Romain Maes suddenly punctured. Fortunately, Sylvère was at hand, and, as a devoted teammate, he passed his wheel to his leader, who as a result lost only a few seconds.

One can only wonder what would have happened if the race leader had been without his teammate and had to change his tyre and inflate it with the hand pump, as the rules stipulated. Antonin Magne and Archambaud would, no doubt, have really put their heads down in an attempt to claim the yellow jersey from him.

It had been another incident-packed day, with numerous punctures and fallers. Were the new duralumin rims the problem? The organisation must have thought so, because messages were sent urgently to Paris asking for fourteen sets of replacement wheels with wooden rims to be dispatched.

Paco finished the stage exhausted but in good heart. He spoke to Spanish journalists waiting to interview him at the finish.

'Look. Now I am feeling much better and I have much more confidence. You will see that in the next mountain stages, I will improve my position. I have come here as an individual rider and I am conscious that the Tour is tougher this way. My experience tells me the importance of determination in this situation and I have no lack of it. From now on I will improve, you will see.'

The following day's stage, stage seven, would take the riders from Aix-les-Bains to Grenoble, over the Galibier, the Giant of the Alps. Paco had goosebumps every time he thought of that colossal mountain. It had a special place in his heart and in the hearts of Spanish fans. Paco had led his teammate, Trueba, over the col in fourth place in the 1930 Tour. On that memorable day, he had firmly introduced himself to the Tour de France and the French fans. In 1933, Trueba had been first to the top and, in 1934, that honour had gone to Fédérico Ezquerra. Paco had relived that momentous day in 1930 many times in his daydreams and on his long and lonely training rides. With Trueba and Ezquerra now back in Spain, did he dare to dream that 1935 might be his year to triumph on the Galibier?

Paco would be climbing the mountain, this year, from the Maurienne valley. In the Tour of 1930, the race had approached the col from the Col du Lautaret side. Paco knew he was riding with more confidence and power each day and the long stage to Grenoble held no fears for him, even though climbing the Galibier from the Maurienne Valley was considered a more difficult proposition as it required an ascent of the Col du Télégraphe first. His legs still had some soreness but he tried to comfort himself with the knowledge that most of the other riders would be feeling the same and the average pace of the day would be much slower than on the previous stages.

As he lay on his hotel bed, gazing at the fan whirring on the ceiling above him, his mind drifted back to that glorious day in July 1930. It was a day that Paco would never forget. Days like that had drawn him back to the Tour de France, even though he knew his friends and family in Sopuerta and Bilbao probably doubted his sanity. But as his eyes became heavy and he stretched out in his soft bed, he felt he had never been more certain of his decision to return to this famous race one final time, and he had every intention of finishing in Paris, at the Parc de Princes Stadium.

Results of Stage 6

Winner: R. Vietto, 6h. 23' 42"
F. Cepeda, 30th, 6h. 34' 1"

Overall: R. Maes, 40h. 53' 27"
F. Cepeda, 62nd, 42h. 30' 45"

17

DAY OF DISASTER

July 11th, Stage 7, Aix-Les-Bains to Grenoble, 229km

The following morning, after a nourishing breakfast, Paco took a moment to write one of the postcards that he liked to send to his friends and fans at the Peña Toreros, in the Café Arriaga, in Bilbao.

> *Aix-les-Bains, 11th July 1935*
>
> *I am addressing everyone to send you a warm greeting from where I am. I suppose you are aware of those early stages which we have ridden at a frightening pace. This was the reason for our slowness and, in part, the unjustified abandonment of our team members. But, to the last, I shall continue to defend myself and I plan to arrive in Paris, provided that there is nothing serious lying in wait for me to upset my wishes.*
>
> *Paco*

It was another early start for the riders, who had two

hundred and twenty-nine tortuous kilometres ahead of them. There was a pensive mood as they set off from the idyllic lakeside town, surrounded by mountain peaks. Those peaks were a reminder to the field of what lay ahead, although, the mountains they would be climbing, within a few hours, would be much bigger.

It would be a hot and undulating day and no one was particularly anxious to start hostilities. There would be plenty of time for that. In previous years, the peloton had taken it easy as far as St Michel du Maurienne, so the first major attacks were not expected until the slopes of the first climb to the Col du Télégraphe. However, only a few kilometres from Aix-les-Bains, on the flat road leading to Chambéry, an unexpected attack came from Benoît Faure, the touriste-routier, from Saint Etienne. This provoked a small split in the peloton and, before anyone knew it, a dozen riders including Vietto, Haendel, Sylvère Maes, Fayolle, Amberg, Neuville, Vervaecke, Prior, Jean Fontenay, Joseph Mauclair and Charles Berty had opened a small gap. Paco had felt invigorated that morning, and had quietly targeted this day, from the start of the race in Paris, to make his mark, inspired by the memories of his ride in 1930. It was a little earlier than he expected but he was alive to the breakaway and he joined this elite and dangerous group.

Aware of the danger, the peloton was riding in small groups, at top speed, through Chambéry, thirty-five kilometres into the stage. They were desperate to bring back these escapees. Paco had noticed that morning that many of the favourites had put on a smaller gear, no doubt, on such a tough day, expecting a slow procession to the foot of the Télégraphe. The Aces were happy to ride with the slower riders this early in the stage, knowing that as soon as they reached the first major climb they would be spat out the back of the peloton. But now they saw this dangerous break getting away, near to Montmélian, the leading riders were getting nervous. Several decided to stop and change their rear wheels, to make use of a higher gear. Others, seeing this, thought it would be a good idea to press on and make a further break. The director waved his red warning flag and some of the following cars stopped abruptly, but then started again. Georges Hubatz, the touriste-routier from Picardy, was taken by surprise. He braked heavily and came to a standstill. A group of tightly-packed following cars concertinaed together. Cries rang out.

'Watch out!'

The French captain, Magne, De Caluwé and at least three others, heads down, crashed into the back of one of the cars. Bodies were catapulted everywhere. Magne did a kind of double somersault, ending up face down on the floor, in a mass of metal. He looked unconscious. The Belgian, Danneels, lay alongside him. His face was streaming with blood. Magne groggily sat up. He was pale and seemed to be slurring his words incoherently. The French team surrounded him and helped him untangle himself from his broken bike. His face was twisted in pain and he was clearly disorientated.

'My cap. Where is my cap?' he mumbled to his concerned teammates.

Romain Maes, seeing his opportunity to further extend his lead over Magne, drove the peloton on at top speed. Of the French team, only Debenne and Speicher followed the main group. But the rest, Leducq, Archambaud, Le Grevès and Merviel, stayed loyal to their captain. They chose to sacrifice their own chances rather than abandon Magne. His fall was a huge blow for the French team but, despite the set back, they were of one mind, namely to get their leader back in the race.

It was a long time before Magne recovered, even a little, from his fall. His elbows, his knees and his right ankle were scraped to the bones. Leducq was magnificent. He comforted and encouraged his friend and, finally, with a helping hand, Magne was able to get back on his feet. He was shaken and tottering but he mounted a new bike which had been brought out for him from the service wagon. Magne's thin face was ashen and he appeared a shadow of the champion he was. How could he possibly recover from this blow? He was on his last legs but, like a true champion, he found the will from somewhere deep inside to continue. The French, assisted by the Germans, Umbenhauer and Stach and the blood-soaked Danneels, coaxed Magne back into the race. The press in the following cars looked on anxiously as this was the man upon whom the hopes of the French nation rested. Somehow they battled on towards the Maurienne valley.

The word 'Maurienne' means wicked river. It comes from the local words mau and riou. There was a real sense of menace as this gently rising road followed the river and wound its way towards the Italian border. The valley was overshadowed, on either side, by imposing, dark, craggy mountains, their faces wild and sheer. The day had certainly darkened for Magne and the French team.

Amongst the crowds which lined the road there was dismay. At Aiguebelle, they watched Magne's group pass in distress. They were more than eleven minutes behind Paco's group. Magne's spirits improved a little when they reached a section where the road seemed almost flat. When they reached St Jean de Maurienne, someone shouted, 'You've got back six minutes.'

But the Tour de France is a cruel race and fifteen kilometres later, Magne had reached Saint Michel de Maurienne, at the foot of the Télégraphe, which then leads to the mighty Galibier. The road steepens quite quickly as it threads its way between the houses on the first slopes of the Télégraphe. Those around Magne hoped and believed he could make it, but every man has his limits and Magne had reached his. He could go no further. The Télégraphe and the Galibier have witnessed many dramatic moments in the past and will do so again, long into the future. Magne's capitulation would be written into the history of these formidable mountain cols. Leaving the town of Saint Michel de Maurienne, Antonin Magne climbed those first slopes of the Télégraphe fighting against the pain. Every turn of the pedals was torture to him. He was on the point of delirium and was weaving across the road, but still he continued, as the notion of abandoning the race plagued him even more than the prospect of continuing. The small groups of spectators lining the road winced at his suffering but his willpower was admirable. Metre by metre, he hauled himself up the side of the mountain. Then, in one fell swoop, his strength abandoned him. It was over.

Magne came to a standstill. Immediately, he was surrounded by his teammates and two journalists, who had been watching this gruesome story unfold.

'I have a deep gash in my right ankle,' Magne spluttered. His face was drained of energy.

'I was climbing with just one leg. I couldn't go on. A man needs more than two legs to climb the Galibier. My teammates have been fantastic.' And then there was silence.

This would be the main story of the day and it would dominate the news in the days ahead. The two pressmen were caught between joy and despair. Joy, in that they could not believe their luck, to have been on the spot when Antonin Magne abandoned the Tour. Despair, in that the man on whom French cycling fans had pinned all their hopes was out of the race. They would telephone their story to their paper later that evening and it would be published in the next edition. That very morning, Magne had appeared on the front page of *Le Miroir des Sports*, confidently drinking from a bottle, resting, ahead of the demi-stage in Geneva. On the thirteenth of July, when *Le Miroir des Sports* was next published, Magne's abandonment would be the subject of the back two pages of the newspaper.

Paco knew nothing of the drama that had unfolded behind

him. He had been involved in his own mini-drama when his front tyre had punctured in Saint Jean de Maurienne. Some riders would jump from their bikes and remove their wheel in an instant and then furiously tear off the tyre in a reflex action. However, Paco was more cautious and circumspect. More haste less speed, he thought. He would remove the wheel and then press his fingers around the smooth rubber, looking for the cause of the puncture. When he replaced the tyre, he again was careful to make sure it was centrally placed and inflated to a good pressure. Once back on the road, he had to work hard, along the false flat of the valley floor, for fifteen kilometres, and then on the first slopes of the Télégraphe, to reach the group he had been with in Aiguebelle. These solo chases would often take their toll on a rider later in the day.

The Galibier is a long and arduous climb. Paco knew that you could not ride hard from the bottom of the Télégraphe and maintain a high tempo to the top. That would be suicidal. You had to pace yourself. He had been climbing steadily, whenever possible, steering towards the shadows cast by the trees, which shielded him from the glare of the baking hot sun. He needed to conserve his energy for the steeper slopes and the desolation ahead that was the Galibier. There were no trees up there; only vast stretches of rocky, desertlike bleakness awaited him. The road to the summit was a trail of misery. Everyone suffered, even the ones who claimed they hadn't. It was etched in the cracks and the crevices of their sunburnt faces. The Galibier is known as one of the Tour's hardest climbs for a reason.

As Paco was reaching the fort at the Col du Télégraphe, with fellow Spaniard, Antonio Prior, the pair were five minutes and fifty seconds behind the leaders, who were on a short but steep descent and nearing the town of Valloire. Paco had been working well with Prior, whilst the lead group continued to be involved in a titanic struggle. Gianello, Camusso and Ruozzi had overtaken Vervaecke and, Benoît Faure, finding his climbing rhythm, was in the mix. However, one of the favourites for the stage, Vietto was in real difficulty. He had dropped back with Alvarez.

On the initial steep ramp out of Valloire, the monstrous Galibier was still hidden from the riders' view. On the left hand side of the road, the rushing waters of the Valloirette were a milky grey. When they reached the small hameau of Les Verneys, the road flattened for a kilometre but, as it did, the enormity of their challenge came into full view; Grand Galibier; sixteen kilometres of rocky road, zig zagging its way up the side of the mountain, to an altitude of two thousand, five hundred and seventy-six metres. From this point, it was hard to imagine a road could even be built to take you across this formidable mountain range. Then once you begin to climb again, you cannot imagine you will ever reach the top. You keep climbing higher and higher. Up, up and up it goes and it seems that the percentage will never let up. At times, there are ramps of fourteen per cent, which means the road rises fourteen metres every hundred metres. Your body warms as you climb but, when you finally reach the top and begin the fast descent, then the sweat cools on your body and a bitter chill gets beneath your skin and into your bones.

The Galibier was first used in the Tour in 1911 and, at the time, was the highest mountain pass in the Tour. There were no homes within twelve kilometres of the summit, and it was easy to see why. It was a desolate and forbidding place, where the locals spoke in strange accents. There had been a mule track over the col since the mid-eighteenth century. This was used mostly by shepherds during the summer months, as well as traders and smugglers who were keen to avoid paying taxes and tolls. In 1879, the military cut out a narrow gravel roadway, to make crossings easier between the departments of Savoie, on the north side, and Hautes-Alpes, on the south side.

They named it Routes des Grandes Communication Number Fourteen. In 1891, the tunnel, three hundred and eighty three metres long, ninety metres below the summit, was finished to avoid the need to cross the col at the highest point.

The col itself is a border and a natural fortification which is cut off from the world, from mid-November to mid-May, by deep snow. By early July, when the Tour arrives, the sun has melted most of the snow, to reveal screes of shale clay on the eastern side and gypsum on the western side. If heavy snow falls in late spring, then a path is dug and riders have to pass between two huge walls of snow and ice. Hundreds of metres below the col, snow patches and ice cling to the road side and the moraine fields. This is a battleground in every sense. This wild and inhospitable mountain range has been sculpted over millions of years of geological chaos. Rocks and minerals which have forced their way upwards, have then been subjected to thousands of years of erosion and glacial movement. That violent struggle continues to this day with the Galibier growing a centimetre each year.

This frontier has also been a place of conflict between nations and kingdoms. France, Spain, Austria-Hungary and the House of Savoie, have all made claims to, and occupied, this rugged place. They built formidable defences amongst the rocks and peaks and men died fighting to defend them. They were destroyed and then rebuilt.

When the Tour de France arrives, a very different battle commences. The conflict is now between the mountain and the riders. The Galibier has humbled some of the toughest riders ever to ride in the Tour. Nevertheless, they take it on regardless and even return again, because to conquer this giant is to achieve a kind of harmony with the landscape; it is a thrill, an intimate and sensuous pleasure. Man, bike and mountain meeting in a single consummation. But it is a beautiful misery, because with the joy of conquering this beast comes pain. Pain in your legs, your back, your arms, your shoulders and your neck. It is an unbearable, aching fatigue from slogging the thirty-four kilometres from the valley bottom. As soon as the race enters the Maurienne Valley, the thoughts of the riders turn to fear and dread.

'It knocks you for six,' were the words of Emile Georget, to the spectators who had gone there by coach and were pressing all around him. On the first ascent in 1911, he was the first rider to have ridden from St Michel, to the summit, and the first to reach the col without putting a foot to the ground. Desgrange promoted the legendary status of this mountain by writing a piece entitled, 'Act of Adoration'.

'Do they not have wings, our riders, who were able to climb to the heights that eagles cannot reach. Oh! Sappey! Oh! Laffrey! Oh! Col du Bayard! Oh! Tourmalet! I would be failing in my duty by not stating that, compared to the vintage Galibier, you are but the pale and common table wine. Before this giant you can but doff your cap and bow low.'

Before setting out in 1913, when the riders climbed the mountain from the southern side, Desgrange warned them, 'From the summit of the Lautaret, you will have to dive down onto the Route du Galibier, which you will start from la Mandette, with a succession of hairpin bends, climbing along the glacier at a slope of fourteen per cent. From La Mandette to the summit of the Galibier is where your main effort will be, as over six of the kilometres are at an average gradient of eleven per cent. What's more, the road is rough and full of potholes. Truly, and I will not stop repeating this, it is a gigantic task, this climbing of the Galibier, through a narrow passageway, traced between two huge walls of snow. Finally, we have the tunnel which marks the highest spot.'

The original route, now known as the Route Ancienne, on the southern side from the Col du Lautaret, was re-routed in 1938. The modern road, used to this day, is longer, measuring eight point six kilometres, but it has a more reasonable gradient of six point eight per cent.

In recent times, a contemporary of Paco, the French rider, Roger Lapébie, talked of the unsurpassed physical agony of riding in the high mountains. He was a solid rider and built like an ox, but the mountains respected no one. 'I was in so much pain when I finished those stages. I had sore hands, sore eyes, sore ankles, a sore arse.'

When asked about his worst memory of the Tour, Lapébie replied, 'When my frame broke and I had to walk. During a descent in the Tour in 1932, I ran into a mule and broke a wheel. I had to walk fifteen kilometres. It was dark when I finished. That was a bad day.' Misfortune and intense pain are a part of Tour de France narratives.

When Ezquerra, one of the three Spaniards who had abandoned on stage five, had crested the Galibier first in 1934, the effort reduced him to tears. He was from Gordejuela, a town not far from Paco's home in Biscay. At the foot of the Télégraph, he was well off the pace. The more experienced Trueba had advised him to stay calm and pace himself so he climbed steadily, reeling in riders as he went. When he caught up with Cañardo, he asked him how many riders were ahead but his compatriot had no idea. As he passed Trueba, on the upper slopes of the Galibier, Trueba told him that only Vietto, the French favourite, was ahead. Nearing the summit, Vietto came into view. The crowds filled the road but he could see that Vietto was being pushed by his French fans. This filled him with anger and he powered on even harder, until he came up alongside the Frenchman. Ezquerra was determined to summit first. For a while, they rode side by side and then, sensing that he was the stronger, the Spaniard pushed on and quickly distanced Vietto. However, a couple of minutes later, when he looked back, Vietto was back on his wheel, having been pushed by the French fans again. This enraged Ezquerra even more and encouraged him to put in an even bigger effort. This time, Vietto had no answer but Ezquerra found his route to the top blocked. The crowds were lashing out at him, trying to impede him. There was only one response. The Biscayan took his pump from his rear pocket and, using it like a machete, slashed a corridor through the lines of spectators. It was a titanic effort, and one that saw him cross the col in first place. He set a new record of one hour, fifty-eight minutes for the ascent of the Galibier from the valley bottom in St Michel. He was to repeat the feat in 1936, living up to the nickname, 'the Eagle', which Desgrange had given him for the way in which he soared in the mountains. His achievements that year were never really acknowledged in Spain, as Franco had mustered his support and Spain was thrown into a bloody civil war. Ezquerra could not return to Spain after the Tour and settled in Pau, close enough to his homeland to hear the bombs exploding. He struggled to make a living as a professional cyclist, relying mainly on his winnings from the Tour de France.

On the Galibier, there is usually at least one moment of drama. It might be on the first slopes, on the hairpins of the Col du Télégraphe, or maybe later, on the rocky wasteland, amongst the snow and ice of the upper reaches of the mountain. Here the closely packed crowds are so close to the riders, they can touch them. Some often do. It is either an enthusiastic slap across the back or sometimes a helpful push, for a local favourite. The noise is deafening and incessant. Both the riders and the following cars have to be on their guard because where huge crowds congregate on the mountains there are genuine hazards. After cresting the cols, many more dangers lie in wait. In fact, this is when the riders are most at risk. Their bodies and their minds are weakened and they have to negotiate the nerve-wracking, zig zag descent from the tunnel. For thirty-three kilometres, to the Col du Lautaret and then towards

Villar-d'Arene, the riders are on the edge of safety. On the rough, gravel roads, through the tunnels and over the bridges of the Romanche, as far as Bourg d'Oisons, this stage has witnessed a series of terrible events. Even those watching from the safety of the roadside are consumed by the drama. They have already had a long day. If they were lucky they may have driven up this perilous road but, more than likely, they would have scaled the mountain on foot, in the early hours of the morning. Then they have to patiently wait for hours, sometimes in rain, hail and snow, but more often in scorching sun, to catch a glimpse of these warriors. There is both excitement and expectation but also absolute alarm and terror as the riders fly past in clouds of dust.

From their high vantage points, on the rocks and patches of moss green grass, the fans have a bird's eye view of the riders as they slowly toil up the steep slopes. At first, they are black dots. They look like marching ants, strung out. They meander this way and that as they try to combat the steepness and fight for their position on the road with the official cars and motorcycles. The road is narrow and in some places barely wide enough for a single vehicle. There are massive, vertical drops at almost every bend. It is utterly gripping. How the multitude of cars, vans, motorcycles and riders manage to negotiate this wild landscape is a miracle. There are always moments of tension between the riders, when insults are exchanged. But, more often than not, the abuse is directed towards the drivers of the official cars, who cause mayhem with their reckless driving. There are plenty of other malicious threats which they have to be overcome, like the rocks and stones, which suddenly move under the tyres, forcing the front or back wheels to slide out. The potholes are death traps when struck at high speed and the steepness and the never ending bends, the heat and the dryness all become insufferable.

On the ascent, each rider seems to be moving in slow

motion. The legs, grinding against the heavy gear are screaming with pain. But on the descent, gravity takes over and the riders are flying, fighting to keep control of their bikes on the uneven surface. No one knows what danger might be lying in wait around the bends. A rock, suddenly dislodged, settles directly in the the racer's line. Then there is always the possibility of a collision. Call them brave or foolhardy, but some riders descend much quicker than others and will try to pass a slower rider on the narrow road. A crash on these gravel tracks would result in serious injuries, not simply cuts and grazes to the bone; more likely broken collar bones, arms, legs or heads. The riders, of course, have to put such thoughts out of their minds and use their skill and every ounce of energy they possess to safely negotiate their way to the bottom. Mostly they just pray.

On this fateful day, as the riders filed up the mountain, Camusso took the lead, but Ruozzi, throwing his bike from side to side, came back with a ferocious attack of his own. It was a monumental battle. The touriste-routier rider, from Nice, had plans to eclipse Vietto who, after a sudden charge, had finally surrendered to the will of the mountain. He was now slogging his way up the final few switch backs towards the tunnel. In the end, it was Ruozzi who claimed the five thousand francs in prize money by going over the col in first place. Vietto had set his mind on claiming that prize but crossed the col in fifteenth position. He was complaining of cramp.

Riding through the cool, blackness of the tunnel was both a blessing and a curse. A blessing in that the road was flat for three hundred and eighty three metres. There was also a brief respite from the burning heat of the sun and the brutal climbing, but the tunnel was also a curse because, in the cold and damp interior, the road became a mass of sticky mud. The rear wheels of the bikes slipped and mud clogged the brakes and gears. When the riders emerged on the other side of the col, the brilliant sunlight, briefly blinded them. They barely had time to adjust their vision to the light before they were hurtling down the dusty and dangerous, twisty descent to the main road, a short distance below the Col du Lautaret. It was a murderous drop. Brakes rattled against the metal rims as if they were about to be blown apart on the rustic track. Camusso, seemed oblivious to the dangers and boldly closed on Benoît Faure. His main target however was Ruozzi and the stage victory.

Paco had lost touch with Prior, five kilometres from the summit and he entered the tunnel three and a half minutes behind him and eighteen minutes behind Ruozzi. Sometimes it was a relief to have the company of a wheel to follow. But on this punishing climb, which wound its way skywards, on what seemed like a meandering and never-ending track, it was a relief to let the wheel go and climb at your own pace. There was a kind of peace to finding your own rhythm, in being alone with your thoughts and being able to concentrate on the stretch of road immediately ahead and not look up and risk crumbling at the stark reality of the kilometres left to climb.

It was always a good feeling to reach the summit, even though, on this occasion, it was tinged with disappointment. When Paco emerged from the tunnel, the realisation came that he had not been able to repeat his Galibier ride from 1930. There would be other opportunities in the Pyrenees, later in the Tour, which Paco thought might be more suited to him. Each day his form had been improving and Paco was reasonably happy with his position. There was still the possibility that he could gain some time, and a higher classification, on the final descent to the finish line. He was tired but he felt that he had not overstretched himself on the climb and there was still a lot of riding to be done; almost one hundred kilometres to the finish, on the the Avenue de Jean Jorgesse, in Grenoble.

At the bottom of the descent from the Galibier, there was

the agonising climb of about two kilometres to the Col du
Lautaret but, once the col was crossed, the descent carried on
at frightening speeds towards La Grave and Le Freney d'Oisons. Ahead of Paco, just before Bourg d'Oisons, Ruozzi had
been finally passed by Camusso who had descended like a
madman. The Italians were known for their daredevil
descending and Camusso had not disappointed the anxious
spectators. They had their hearts in their mouths. He was now
on on a better road surface and was, almost certainly, heading
for the stage victory.

Further back, Romain Maes in his yellow jersey, and the
Italian, Vignoli, who had been riding together for some time,
suddenly touched wheels. Both riders were brought heavily to
the ground. The few spectators that were present on the road
side rushed to their aid and a car from *Le Petit Parisen* newspaper screeched to a halt. Both riders were helped to their feet
but only Maes, perhaps inspired by the yellow jersey on his
back, seemed interested in rejoining the race. With help from a
spectator, who had picked up his bike, which was surprisingly
undamaged, he remounted and rode off, no doubt pumping
with adrenalin. The Italian was not so fortunate. He was
moaning and clutching his left arm. His collar bone was probably broken and his body felt shattered. His race was done. He
climbed into one of the following sedans and was driven to
hospital in Grenoble. A little further on, a car had crashed into
a rock on a sharp bend and its driver had split open his fore-
head. There was also news that Danneels, who had struggled
throughout the afternoon with his bloodied wounds heavily
bandaged, had finally been forced to abandon. The Queen's
Stage of the Tour de France was turning into a bloodbath.

18

THE FINAL DESCENT

Tour de France, Thursday 11th July 1935, Stage 7, Aix-Les-Bains to Grenoble

On that savage Thursday afternoon, as Paco started his descent of the Galibier, the Cepeda family, at home in Sopuerta, were taking their siesta. The postcard that Paco had written to his family from Charleville had not yet arrived, so the father and brothers had relied on snippets from Spanish newspaper reports for their race updates.

Augustín had continued to struggle to accept his son's decision to return to professional cycling. He did not understand it and he could see no sense in it. But he was also plagued by regrets that he had not found it in his heart to give his son his blessing when he had left for Paris. He was a proud man who found compromise hard and so he had found it difficult to enjoy Paco's final days in Sopuerta. Primitivo could sense his father's worry and thought about trying to raise his mood, but he was wary of opening the old man's wounds. Paco would be home soon, he thought. He would ride triumphantly into Paris, he would announce his retirement from bike racing, return to the family home in Sopuerta, and father and son would be reconciled.

Rioupéroux, 4:30pm

S uddenly, Antonio Prior heard that agonising squealing of brakes and the clatter and scraping of metal against the road but, by the time he had the presence of mind to look back over his left shoulder, all he could see was a cloud of dust and what seemed like two vehicles stopped in the middle of the road. He had instinctively reached for his brake levers on hearing what he assumed to be a crash of some sort, but he really had no idea what had happened.

Prior thought he had been travelling at at least forty-five kilometres per hour but he was probably riding closer to sixty. Even though he had braked, the road had continued its down-ward trajectory to the right, so the mayhem and confusion that lay behind him rapidly disappeared from view. Prior relaxed his grip on the brake levers and his bike gathered momentum again. He was soon surrounded by the other riders from the small group. There was Leducq and Pélissier but there was no sign of Paco Cepeda. The riders looked at one another.

'What happened?' 'Where is little Cepeda?'

There was no response. Simply shrugs and looks of puzzlement. This had been a day of punctures and crashes and pain, intolerable pain at times. This terrible stage would end in just over an hour, but bodies and minds were exhausted. No matter how cautiously a rider rode, his race could be over in a second, as Magne had found out earlier in the day. Prior hoped Cepeda's race was not over. If he had crashed, hopefully, he would be back on his feet and already rejoining the race, but now someone else was on the attack and Prior did not want to lose contact with this group. At this stage in the race, it was every man for himself. There was no time for sentiment. Prior, like the others, had his mind on the general classification, so he pressed on for Grenoble regardless.

Prior was wrong. Paco would not be rejoining the race. His bloodied body lay motionless and stretched out in the road. The drivers and the passengers from the two cars, which had screeched to a standstill in the wake of the crash, were standing over him. There was panic and confusion. A cloud of dust filled the road. Some of the men were shouting in Spanish and others in French. There was now a posse of officials and locals around the stricken body of the cyclist. More and more people were running to the scene, from both directions, to see what all the commotion was about. Slowly, the dust kicked up by the crash began to settle.

'I'll run for the doctor,' shouted a voice.

'He needs the hospital,' cried another.

A woman covered the eyes of her two young children and hurriedly led them away from the tragic scene. Finally, several men carefully lifted Paco and placed him in one of the two sedans. Blood was seeping from a head wound and his body was limp. He was laid out across the back seat and covered with a blanket. His bike was bundled into the second car and, without any more delay, both vehicles sped off in the direction of Grenoble. There was a small pool of blood on the road where Paco had lain. The whole terrible event had happened in a split second and, now it was over, that corner of the road had returned to its usual calm. The small crowd was now muted, dumbstruck and shocked by the suddenness and the gravity of what they had witnessed. One or two began to walk away from the scene while others stood in small groups, trying to make sense of what they had seen.

Suddenly someone shouted. 'Watch out! Watch out! Riders coming!'

Two riders came flying through the bend and then another, completely oblivious to the terrible event that had happened there minutes earlier.

Paco was rushed to La Tronche hospital, on the outskirts of Grenoble, where he was taken to a small and spartan room. When he arrived, he was still unconscious. Nurses cleaned and treated his cuts and grazes and bandaged his head. Two doctors arrived, examined him and, after a brief consultation, decided to assess his condition in the following hours.

With the stage completed, there was little talk of Paco's accident amongst the riders that evening at dinner. He had been taken to hospital, his condition was not thought to be serious and that was all. There had been no official statement regarding his condition from the race organisers but it was clear he would not return to the race. Talk that evening around the supper tables was mainly about Magne's abandonment and Camusso's victory. The newspapers were preparing those stories for the nation, as well as reaction to Danneels abandonment, which meant a French victory was now extremely unlikely. Ever hopeful, the French media and fans would get behind Vietto, but the Belgian, Romain Maes, had strengthened his position in the lead and he was now the red hot favourite to wear the yellow jersey all the way to Paris.

Privately, there were more complaints about the new metal rims and some of the riders grumbled about the number of punctures which had plagued the race from the first day. There was some speculation that the accidents to Cepeda and Vignoli could have been connected to the duralumin rims. Rumours were also circulating that some of the Aces had taken their concerns to the organisers and had demanded a return to the wooden rims. The response was that the replacement wooden rims, that had previously been ordered to be sent from Paris, would finally arrive for the following day's stage.

The next morning, with Paco fighting for his life in a hospital, only a few kilometres from the start of the stage, the race continued, from Grenoble to Gap, and, for the riders and the organisation, the circus roadshow continued. Thoughts of Paco and his condition were set to one side.

PART FOUR

THE SEARCH FOR THE TRUTH

19

THE AFTERMATH

The morning after the accident, the Cepeda family received the news every family of a professional cyclist dreads, in a telegram, from one of the Spanish newspapers. Paco's father, Augustín, and his two brothers, Gerardo and Primitivo, travelled to the editorial offices of *Excelsius* newspaper, in Bilbao. The newspaper had arranged a telephone call with the director of the hospital in Grenoble, in the hope that there might be an update on Paco's condition.

'How is Cepeda?' asked the editor.

'His condition is now beginning to worry us,' came the reply. 'It is not easy to make a prognosis at the moment.'

'But we were told that the situation was not so serious.'

'On the contrary. I'm afraid it is serious. This morning a trepanation has been carried out.'

'Has it been successful?'

'Well, these head injuries always provide us with the answers fairly quickly. For the moment, we cannot provide you with any further information. Only the fact that Monsieur Cepeda's injury is something that needs care.'

'Thank you. We will call again tomorrow.'

The editor put down the phone. There was silence in the office. Everyone looked at one another. Their eyes revealed their thoughts and a gloom descended on the room. The father looked pale and the brothers bowed their heads.

'Don't give up hope,' the editor said, placing his hand reassuringly on Augustín's shoulder. 'We must have faith in the medical science and, with God's help, they will protect Paco from the danger around him. Hopefully in the morning the news will be more optimistic.'

Augustín looked doubtful. His brothers looked at their father but could find no words to encourage him. They felt helpless. Their brother was lying in a hospital bed, many miles away, surrounded by strangers and they wanted to be by his side, to hold his hand and to tell him that everything would be fine and soon they would be back at home, in the Biscayan summer sunshine, enjoying their mother's cooking.

Adding to the family's anxiety, Spanish newspapers struggled to establish the absolute truth regarding the causes of the accident and also published conflicting reports about Paco's condition. While *Excelsius* published a transcript of the telephone conversation with the director of the hospital, *El Pueblo Vasco* carried the headline, 'The Spaniard Cepeda's condition is satisfactory.' It reported Paco's injury was satisfactory and the pains he had been suffering were almost gone. The report also claimed that the rider was annoyed because the accident had happened just when he was getting into shape.

Similarly, *La Gaceta Del Norte* reported that Paco's condition was quite satisfactory. It said his Tour de France was now over, despite his eagerness to reach Paris. According to their report, Paco had lost consciousness after the fall and it was believed he had fractured his skull, but the injury was not serious and he would begin to recover after a couple of weeks. He had had a quiet night and had recovered consciousness. He had a fever, which had caused some delirium, but only for brief moments.

No complications were expected and his family had been given very satisfactory news at noon. He was considered to be out of danger. Nevertheless, his mother and sister had left for Grenoble.

El Mundo Deportivo, the Barcelona newspaper, was more circumspect and reported that concern for Paco was growing. The Spanish community in Grenoble had rallied behind him and were covering his expenses in hospital. They had paid for the operation to save his life and were raising money for any other expenses the rider or his family might incur as a result of the terrible accident. It added that Paco's condition had worsened and his family had been advised to travel to his bedside in the event of the worst possible outcome. On page four, the newspaper also reported that Paco, along with Figueras, had wanted to abandon the race on the same day that Trueba, Ezquerra and Cañardo had left the race. It was reported Paco had lost all confidence in the hope of achieving a good position in the general classification because his knees had been swollen since the second stage, owing to the terrible cobblestone roads of northern France. He felt he could no longer maintain thirty kilometres per hour for longer than ten kilometres. Finishing the stages had been a huge effort for him. The newspaper asserted he and Figueras had only continued because both riders feared, if they abandoned the race, people would view their abandonment as clear evidence that, all along, they had been in a conspiracy with the other Spanish riders. The newspaper claimed both riders had felt they had been emotionally out of the race since the fourth stage. Cepeda's knees looked like footballs.

ABC, from Madrid, reported Paco had been a victim of his own enthusiasm. Its reporters had spent the night in the hospital and claimed Paco had been mostly delirious but occasionally recovered consciousness. The doctors had decided to operate because they were not optimistic about his condition.

On Sunday the fourteenth of July, the reports about Paco's condition were even more confused. In San Sebastián, news was circulating that he had died. Señor Gervais, the Spanish selector, was quick to call Grenoble and he was told that, not only was the news false, the truth was Cepeda was much better. The intervention of the surgeons had been quite normal and the surgery had been quite satisfactory. He had spent a quiet night in the hospital and his pains had lessened. He had recovered consciousness completely. Sometimes the fever made him semi-conscious but those occasions were only momentary. The only danger was if there were complications, like an infection, but these were not expected. *Excelsius* reported a slight improvement, but a conflicting report, from another source in Paris, said Paco's condition was still very serious and his brother had arrived in Grenoble. *El Pueblo Vasco* stated that the doctors were optimistic Paco's determined nature would dominate and, unless there were complications, he should make a complete recovery. However, in complete contrast, according to sources from *Paris Soir*, Paco had not recovered consciousness and his doctors had lost all hope of saving him. It was feared he would not survive the night.

These conflicting newspaper stories put a huge strain on the family, who were in no position to rush to their son's bedside. They had very little money and certainly did not have sufficient funds to travel by boat, or train, to Grenoble. The store they owned allowed them a living slightly above the average worker in Sopuerta, but they did not have enough money to face this terrible situation alone.

On the fifteenth of July, *El Mundo Deportivo*, one of the few Spanish dailies to be printed on a Monday, finally ended speculation when it carried the distressing headline:

'SHORTLY AFTER EIGHT, CEPEDA HAS DIED'

The newspaper reported that Francisco Cepeda had died peacefully, on July the fourteenth, at eight-fifteen in the evening. His eldest brother Gerardo had arrived from Spain, at three in the afternoon, and with the Spanish coach, Señor Gervais, had been at his bedside until Paco quietly passed away. Some members of the Spanish community in Grenoble had kept a vigil at the hospital. It was a Spanish journalist, covering the Tour, who communicated the dreadful news to his teammates and Spanish officials. Naturally, the news spread quickly amongst the riders who knew Paco well and held him in such high regard, not only for his skill as a rider but also for his friendly and happy-go-lucky character.

Crashes were common in cycle races, with riders sometimes receiving serious injuries, but no one had ever died riding in the Tour de France. Adolphe Hélière, a 19-year-old amateur rider, drowned after he went for a swim in the Mediterranean, on a rest day in Nice, during the 1910 Tour de France, but Paco became the first rider to die following a crash during a stage. It was a dark day for the Tour de France.

On Tuesday the sixteenth of July, *Excelsius* reported that the trepanation carried out on Paco had, in principle, been successful, but he had not recovered consciousness before he died peacefully. They claimed if the Tour organisers had more humanity, Cepeda's accident would never have happened and said there was certainly a lack of sensitivity shown towards the individuals and the touristes-routiers. The journalist stressed riders, like Cepeda, had not been properly assisted. There was not even an ambulance available for them. Paco had been taken to hospital in a private car, and this had not helped his chances of survival.

Gerardo Cepeda was the only family member able to make the long and difficult journey to France. He at least was with Paco in his final hours. He thanked the Spanish community for the care and the financial support which had been given to his brother. They had been so attentive to him in the three dramatic days he had spent fighting for his life.

Cepeda died on Sunday in the hospital in Grenoble', *Excelsius* published on its front page. 'Today in the regional capital of France, the ill-fated rider's funeral ceremony will take place, in the hospital, in the presence of the Prefect of the Isère Department, before the remains are transferred, by train, to Hendaye, arriving there probably on Thursday.'

La Gaceta del Norte echoed the terrible news and gave another series of details relating to his death. 'Yesterday evening, Cepeda died in hospital, despite the best efforts of the doctors to save him. Around him at his death were his brother and the Spanish selector Mr Gervais.' This newspaper had doubts about the official story. They asked how it was possible that an experienced rider, like Cepeda, could have fractured his head in an accident of this kind. Falls like his were extremely common. The newspaper speculated that the cars around the riders may have, in some way, contributed to the accident, although they admitted this was only an idea and there was no actual evidence this had happened. To many, the situation seemed incomprehensible, as Cepeda was one of the most experienced riders in the peloton. He was also always so meticulous in his planning and his preparation.

Some rumours were circulating that Paco's skull had not been fractured but that, after the surgery, he had contracted meningitis. An infection may have finally killed Paco, but what seemed most likely was that, contrary to several newspaper reports, Paco had never regained consciousness after his fall.

20

A FAMILY'S GRIEF

I t was impossible to tell exactly how the Cepeda family was feeling after the news of the death of their beloved son filtered back to the sleepy town of Sopuerta, so far from Grenoble. Of course, with two sons racing, one at a professional level, Augustín and Tomasa had lived with the possibility of hearing, one day, that one of their sons had been injured in a crash or a fall, but fatalities in the sport were relatively rare and, anyway, what good could come from dwelling on such terrible thoughts. But now a fatality had happened, for the first time in the Tour de France, and it fell upon journalist Juan García to make the journey to Sopuerta and intrude upon the family's grief.

At the end of a busy day, Juan left his office and battled through the rush hour traffic and began the long journey, along the coast, from San Sebastián to Bilbao, into the heart of the Basque Country, in search of the small iron mining town of Sopuerta. He made the journey with a heavy heart and a little apprehension. He loved his job and this was an opportunity to cover a major story involving one of Spain's elite cyclists. There was no greater satisfaction for a reporter than to be at the heart of a story as it unfolded, and yet this assignment would require him to inflict more agony on the grief-stricken Cepeda family. Who could possibly imagine the scale of their pain? Their son, cruelly and suddenly taken from them in such terrible circumstances.

By the time he arrived at the home of Francisco Cepeda it was dark. Since the announcement of Paco's untimely death, the Cepeda family home had been shrouded in sorrow. The ground floor shutters had remained closed and the curtains drawn. Residents of Sopuerta removed their hats in sympathy for the family's suffering and passed in quiet contemplation.

As Juan brought his car to a halt outside the house, the headlights silhouetted a small group of young men who had gathered on the corner of the main street. Several racing bicycles leant against the wall of the house. Friends from the local cycling community and neighbours, he assumed. They stood in sombre silence outside the house, in which Paco had lived for the entirety of his short life. These young men formed a kind of guard of honour, protecting the Cepeda family in their time of grief.

The journalist was now the centre of attention. Reaching for his hat and briefcase, which lay on the passenger seat, he took a deep breath, braced himself and opened the car door. Nervously adjusting his hat, he slowly made his way to the front door of the two-storey, corner house. He felt the accusing eyes of the men but no words were exchanged. He was a stranger in this small town, which had been dealt a terrible blow by the sudden loss of their beloved friend and neighbour. Juan acknowledged the young men, by tipping his hat, but he looked at no one in particular. He was aware of the thick cigarette smoke in the warm evening air and the barking of a dog in the distance. He knocked on the door, heard quiet footsteps approaching, and waited anxiously until the door opened.

A solemn-faced young man, Primitivo, one of Paco's brothers, beckoned the journalist inside. Juan removed his hat and carefully placed it on the hat stand in the hallway. From somewhere inside the house, he could hear the soft sound of someone sobbing. Primitivo led the journalist through the dark hallway and into the kitchen, where he was greeted by two more young men, and a young girl, brothers and a sister of the deceased, he assumed, and the father, Augustín. His first impression of the father was that he was overwhelmed with grief. To see the head of the household, normally an unshakable man, now utterly broken, shook Juan to the core. Regaining some composure, he asked after the mother.

'How and where is your mother?'

'She is upstairs, half dead on hearing this terrible news. Losing her beloved son is only the beginning of her pain and grief. It goes deeper. She has lost hope. There is no end in sight to her suffering,' replied Primitivo.

This haunting image of a mother's despair was followed by a profound silence. The journalist, to whom words normally came easily, was now lost for words.

Finally, the brothers, Gregorio, Fernando and Primitivo came to his rescue.'You are the first to come and offer condolences in such painful times,' said Primitivo. 'I am very sorry Señor Garcia but I fear our overwhelming grief and sadness will not allow us to tell you the story of our brother, Paquito.'

However, they were wrong. Without any prompting from Juan, they began to tell the whole story, driven by an outpouring of love and admiration for their brother.

Gregorio, the emotion clearly evident in his quivering voice began.

'At home, we called him Paquito. It was Paquito who was always the happiest one in our house and there is nothing that can fill the gap that has been left. As brothers, we adored him, because he was good and because he was honest with us. He brought dignity to the family and to the town with his fame and his popularity.'

'I have read that he was the municipal judge of Sopuerta. Is this true?'

'Yes sir, he was,' answered the father. This was the first time that Augustín had spoken. 'He was elected unanimously by the town. There are few people who are as honest and have such good manners and morals as our son. My son was in bed every night by ten o'clock. He liked neither parties nor love affairs. His love of cycling came first, and then his work in the shop and in the Agency of the Bank of Biscay. These responsibilities took up all hours of the day. Recently, he had also started a correspondence course. He was studying to be an electrical engineer. He loved it and he was achieving the best grades. I was so happy that he had started to study, mainly in the hope that he had lost his desire for cycling.'

'Did you not like that he was a cyclist?'

'A professional cyclist? No. I didn't like it. He didn't have much luck on the road because he was too selfless. He was too much of a gentlemen. The Tour de France was the true delusion. It consumed his strength and will, and you can see why. Poor Paquito! My poor, poor son. Fallen there on the side of the road! It makes no sense. It's against the natural order. A father should not outlive his son.'

With those fateful words, Augustín's voice began to break. The realisation of his loss unleashed a torrent of grief and sadness which utterly consumed him. He began to sob uncontrollably and his raw emotion moved everyone in the room.

Gathering himself, the father continued, 'I never wanted it to be. I said it again and again. You are going to die! You are going to die! I know I said it because I had been a bit sensitive for a long time, but now I have been proved right. How horrible! How horrible!'

Throughout his career, Little Paco, as he was known by

everyone in his town, wrote cards to his parents, whenever he could, to tell them which towns and cities he would be at during rest days so they could write to him. Augustín walked slowly to a dresser where some of Paco's silver cups and trophies gleamed in the lamplight. He reached for a postcard.

'This was the last we heard from him.'

The card was dated the ninth of July.

Dear parents and siblings: a hug from your son.

A final message. Five days later, he was dead. The family first heard about the accident from the radio. Their anxiety rapidly grew, owing to the conflicting reports about the seriousness of Paco's injuries in the first days after the accident. Gerardo, the eldest brother, had left immediately for Grenoble. On Monday, both through the press and from official sources, the crushing news arrived. Tomasa, the mother, had prayed night and day, for three days, hoping against hope that her son would recover, but on hearing the news she was completely overwhelmed by it. Her children feared she would not be able to bear the pain of seeing her son's body again or withstand the agony of the funeral.

'Are you going to bring the body home?'

'We would like to, although we fear, for us, it will be an impossible financial strain.'

Suddenly, the phone rang in the hall. It was Gregorio who went to answer it. When he returned a few moments later, his eyes were moist with tears.

'They're already bringing him. They're already bringing him.'

The words that followed could barely be heard because Gregorio had slumped against the wall, and spoken through uncontrollable sobs.

Everyone remained silent at this latest news. It was

assumed that the body was going to arrive in Irun, and the brothers would have to travel there to receive the coffin. It later transpired that the generous Spanish community in Grenoble had taken responsibility for the costs of transporting Paco's remains from the hospital to its final resting place in Sopuerta.

'Mother knows nothing of this yet,' said Primitivo 'How do we possibly tell her?'

'She will die,' said Espe, the young sister, who until that moment had remained silent. She had been sitting in a corner of the room with her head in her hands. 'When she sees Paquito's body she will die.'

'Hush!' pleaded Primitivo. 'Mother will hear us. We must be quiet.'

Juan felt he could intrude on the family's suffering no longer. He rose quietly and placed his notebook and pen in his briefcase. He shook hands with the father and the brothers and made his way into the hallway. From the front room, he could hear more sobbing. Stepping into the darkened room, he saw a young woman weeping silently.

She told the reporter her name was Teresita Nistal. She was the cousin of the Cepeda siblings, with whom she had always lived. She had lost her mother when she was a very young child and, following that loss, her father, had emigrated to America, leaving her behind. Now, after hearing the news of the death of her cousin, she had travelled from Bilbao, where she worked in a drug store on Astarloa Street.

'They all love me in this house, everyone, but Paquito loved me the most. Our relationship was something special, something that I have now lost, forever. Paco never wanted to see me sad. He defended me, even if I wasn't right. And if he knew of anyone saying anything dishonourable about me, owing to me not having family, he would have killed them. A little while ago, I had an appendicitis operated on, and there wasn't a single day that he didn't ask after me. Every time he passed through Bilbao, he would visit me. He would take me to the theatre or we would go for a walk. The owners of the drug store loved him so much, because he was so kind and loving towards everyone. Even a young boy in the house keeps asking, 'Where is Paco? When is Paco coming?' Everyone, everyone loved him. I cannot believe that I will never see him again.'

With that she buried her face in her handkerchief and returned to her sobbing. Juan left her to her grief and stepped from the forlorn house and out into the pitch blackness.

Tributes poured in for Paco over the following days. Paco was referred to as a dedicated rider, and an exceptional person. With his death, Spanish cycling had lost one of its outstanding gentlemen. The Barcelona paper *La Vanguardia* described Paco as, 'an optimistic person and a very scientific rider. He was methodical and meticulous, and in every race he made a deep study of the road, the tactics to be applied, and the gears to be used. He succeeded more because of his belief in his preparations, than because of his physical condition.'

El Pueblo Vasco, in Bilbao, the newspaper to whom Paco had been reporting regularly throughout the Tour, wrote, 'Spanish cycling has lost an exemplary man and Basque sport an enthusiastic rider. His most remarkable virtue was his professional self-esteem. His most intimate yearning, the spread of cycling throughout Spain. He was extremely modest, and his serious and straight-forward character gave him great moral value. Only recently, he had become the Justice of the Peace in his home town, which is proof of his integrity and prestige.'

El Mundo Deportivo commented that although Paco was not a rider of extraordinary class, he was intelligent and full of professional honesty. Tenacity and enthusiasm were his main virtues and he had only ever abandoned a race owing to unavoidable physical circumstances. The Biscayan rider was a true sportsman and one of the best climbers in Europe.

L'Auto, *L'Intransigeant*, *Paris-Soir*, and other French newspapers, praised Paco, recognising his virtues of eagerness, friendliness and sportsmanship. Journalist Gaston Bénac, who worked for *Paris Soir*, knew Paco personally. He travelled to Spain each year, working for Henri Desgrange, to negotiate contracts with riders for the Tour and he had recruited Paco earlier that year. To Bénac, Paco was a true role model for sportsmen, always determined, optimistic and good-humoured. In contrast to Vicente Trueba, Spain's most celebrated rider, Bénac remembered his negotiations with Paco were always polite and straightforward. He was always assured of a warm welcome and he would never forget Paco's beaming smile each time he met him. He fondly recalled sitting down with Paco in the room where his gleaming trophies took pride of place and the ease of their contract talks. Paco would have ridden the Tour for pure pleasure, whereas Trueba was always troublesome when it came to contract negotiations. Bénac thought Trueba was dishonest and badly advised. On the other hand, visiting Paco and his family in Sopuerta was always a delight. He remembered clearly how grateful Paco was when he brought the news of his invitation to the twenty-ninth Tour de France.

'Please tell Monsieur Desgrange how happy I am for thinking of me. I am so happy about riding the Tour again. I consider it to be the pinnacle of my career. Rest assured, I will do everything in my power to be worthy of receiving this invitation.'

If only all Bénac's negotiations could have been that straightforward. Paco was a modest young man and when people met him, they could not help but warm to his light-hearted and generous nature. Bénac recalled their final meeting, in Aix-Les-Bains, before the start of that terrible stage.

'How are you going?' asked Bénac.

'I am good for the Galibier, but I will be better in the Pyrenees,' replied Paco, half in Spanish, half in French.

And now, just over a week later, the little Spaniard's body was being transported to the railway station and a funeral was being prepared in Sopuerta.

The Cepeda family was in despair but, being an honest and dutiful family, they wrote a letter of thanks to *El Pueblo Vasco* and other newspapers, for providing them with information about the accident and their beloved son's death. They also wished to thank all the people who had sent messages of condolences. Paco's body was due to arrive at Sopuerta on Thursday 19th of July, in the afternoon and, following a requiem mass, would be taken to the cemetery of San Cristóbal, on the outskirts of the town, the following day, at six in the evening.

The family had received no direct communication from Henri Desgrange or his newspaper. A snippet had appeared on page three of *L'Auto*, paying tribute to Paco. It simply stated that, 'he was a shy and cautious boy who had been exemplary in his correctness. He always showed his best spirit and he seemed to find great pleasure in the pursuit of this sport that would finally end his life.'

There was a suggestion from a sympathetic reader to one newspaper that, 'some day, a merciful hand will build a cross at the point where the accident happened, at which, in future Tours, riders might stop and pay their respects,' but nothing had been endorsed by the organisers. A Spanish journalist made claims for a sculpture to be located in the headquarters of the Sociedad Ciclista Bilbaina, Cepeda's last team.

Perhaps the most poetic and heart-felt farewell came in *Paris Soir*, from Bénac.

'Poor unfortunate Cepeda,' he wrote. 'A brave competitor from the mounts of Biscay! You did not arrive either in the Pyrenees or in Sopuerta, where a mother weeps for a cyclist who was a pure amateur, who loved the mountains and who lived only for climbing and climbing the passes. In a small corner of France, you found yourself face to face with death and although you tried, you could not overcome it. Those who were your companions and opponents in this ordeal drive on, seeing the Latin Sea on the Cote d'Azur, with the crepe of an armband. You will never know the finish of this Tour of which you have been the victim.'

Bénac appealed for compensation for the Cepeda family, since it seemed clear to him that the accident had been caused by a technical problem. He claimed that Desgrange had informed him about an insurance policy but there was confusion as to whether the Tour riders were actually covered. The journalist also criticised the lack of assistance given by the Spanish consulate and Spanish team delegates.

As promised, there was a minute's silence before the Nice to Cannes stage on the sixteenth of July. The riders stood in silence alongside their bicycles. The muscles tensed in their faces. Their expressions were grim. They lowered their heads and were still. Most knew Paco well and respected him. They admired his courage, had benefited from his kindness and laughed at his good humour. As they stood in silence, some remembered special moments. For example, when he played the matador after supper, on warm summer evenings. Riders would take it in turns to charge at him. Their fingers, protruding from their heads, were the horns of the bull. At the last minute, Paco would nimbly step to one side, with an elegant sweep of a chequered table cloth and stamp his foot in triumph. There would be thunderous cheers of, 'Olé!' from those watching.

Others who did not know Paco so well, might have thought, in that minute of silence, about the imminent dangers they might also be facing that day, and later in the week, when they would be plunging from Pyrenean summits, on narrow roads, at breakneck speeds. If they had any sense, they would quickly cast Paco's misfortune from their minds, otherwise they might never race again.

The Spanish riders had also agreed to contribute part of their benefits towards the transfer of Paco's remains to Spain. Some of the foreign riders would do likewise. The Chairman of the Spanish Cycling Committee had sent a telegraph to the few Spanish riders still competing in the race, advising them to abandon, as a sign of respect for the death of Cepeda. However, the riders did not follow his advice. They thought it would be better to remain in the race. They felt they needed to continue to uphold the reputation of the Spanish people, particularly in the light of the earlier abandonments.

On the eighteenth of July, Paco's body was still in Bordeaux but his funeral in Sopuerta had been scheduled for late afternoon of the twentieth. On the morning of the eighteenth, Gerardo met with Señor Gervais, while the remaining brothers made their way, by bus, to Amara bus station, in San Sebastián. There, some locals drove them to Hendaye. They waited, but Paco's body still did not arrive. Later they were assured the body would arrive in St-Jean-de-Luz, where it would be transferred to a car that would then take it home to Sopuerta.

Finally, at seven in the evening, Paco's casquette arrived at the border. In San Sebastián, a procession formed from the Kursaal to La Perla del Océano. At La Concha beach, Paco received an emotional farewell. There was a sea of wreaths and flowers from local well-wishers who had known Paco and followed his cycling career. Gerardo expressed his thanks for the affection shown for both his brother and himself. The Montero brothers and other cycling enthusiasts and fans from San Sebastián then rode alongside the coffin to the limits of the province.

On the afternoon of the twentieth, the day of the funeral, a huge crowd gathered in Sopuerta, around the Cepeda house.

Special buses had brought people in from Bilbao. Hundreds of cyclists and many representatives of cycling clubs in Biscay, Gipuzkoa and Cantabria, rode their bikes to the funeral, to pay homage to Paco. Once near the Cepeda house, they dismounted and walked solemnly with their bikes, their brows furrowed and their faces strained. They lined the road between the Cepeda house, the church and the cemetery of San Cristóbal, three or four deep in places. The men wore their Sunday best and many of the women were veiled in black. Mr. Ernest Lafont, Minister of Physical Education for the French Government, represented France at the funeral, but no one came from the offices of *L'Auto* or the Tour organisation.

In the beautiful, ancient church of San Pedro, Paco's remains lay in a coffin, flanked by eight candles, four on each side. Vivid bouquets of flowers and elaborate wreathes adorned it, and the wall behind the altar burst with the colours and the fragrance of the summer. This was in stark contrast to the mourners; the men in their dark suits, and the women in their black dresses and veils, many weeping and sobbing, over-whelmed with grief. It was a sad and sombre sight.

Following the requiem mass, the mourners processed behind the coffin, as Paco made his final journey from the church, down the hill, past the family home, to the nearby cemetery. Vicente Trueba was one of the pallbearers. The mourners walked slowly and solemnly in rows of twenty. Priests from every village and town in the region had come to offer their prayers and support for the Cepeda family. They rever-ently walked amongst the mourners and, together, they filled the road. It was difficult to say how many were present but there must have been well over a thousand in attendance. Eventually, they reached the iron gates, marking the entrance to the small, walled cemetery and, in the far left hand corner, Paco was finally laid to rest.

The funeral may have brought some closure to the Cepeda

family regarding the terrible events of the eleventh of July, which led to the untimely death of their cherished son but, in the weeks and months that followed, there was no let up in the speculation around Paco's crash. Each time a report was published on the subject, the wound was opened again.

Two days after the funeral, Mr Gervais visited the Spanish riders in Luchon and Antonio Prior gave him the following document:

'Those of us who have signed below, certify that we were present at the fall of the unfortunate Cepeda, but did not give the accident importance at the time and carried on with our ride. Of course, as far as we were concerned, it was a normal fall.' Signed at Bagneres de Luchon, 22nd July 1935. A Prior, A Leducq.

In the same document, written in French. 'I saw that he was in my group but I did not see him fall.' Signed by R Le Grevès, and Charles Pélissier.

There were many who thought this document supported the case that Desgrange and the Tour organisation had not been negligent, despite the criticism from many journalists about the new duralumin rims. It also seemed to many, that Henri Desgrange and the Tour organisation had turned their backs on the Cepeda family, following the accident. In complete contrast, the Cepeda family were magnanimous in their desperate hour of need. Monsieur Gervais, *L'Auto's* correspondent in San Sebastián, received a letter from Augustín Cepeda which was to be passed on to Monsieur Desgrange.

Sopuerta, Biscay, 23rd July 1935

Mr. Gervais,

The undersigned, father, brothers and sisters of the unfortunate rider, Francisco Cepeda, beg you to be kind enough to send a letter to Paris, from you, so that, at the moment when the Tour de France ends, you, on our behalf, give our sincere thanks to the organisers and riders of this race, for the show of sorrow they have given to our whole family.

Once again, we express our thanks and we remain your servants and friends.

Agustín Cepeda, Gregorio, Primitivo, Fernando, Esperanza, Teresa Nistal, Gerardo Cepeda.

The Cepeda family eventually received three hundred and eighty-three francs from the Tour organisers, their son's meagre winnings from the race, but no compensation was forthcoming. It turned out that Paco was not insured. Reports which had circulated previously, about there being an insurance policy for the riders, proved to be untrue. There was not even a letter of condolence to the family. The only acknowledgement of Francisco Cepeda's death by Henri Desgrange were those few lines written in his newspaper, on the sixteenth of July.

It seemed that Henri Desgrange went out of his way not to acknowledge Paco's death. He was presumably desperate to avoid any unfavourable coverage of his race, as well as accusations of blame. Some suggestions circulated that Paco's parents would have to sell their family home and business to pay for the funeral and burial expenses. Paco's position as the Municipal Judge in his district was only part-time and did not pay well. Primitivo, Paco's younger brother, was angry about the absence of any financial compensation from the Tour and the fact that Desgrange did not attend the funeral or offer his personal condolences. He confirmed that the family had written to the Tour asking for the insurance coverage but, in return, had only received a copy of a clause, in which the organisers stated they were not liable for any injuries received by the riders, and, furthermore, would not even be liable for any damages caused to third parties.

It was a wretched time for the Cepeda family and the community of Sopuerta but, a few days after the funeral, a letter arrived at the Cepeda household which would raise their beleaguered spirits. It was addressed to Gerardo, so his father handed it to him. When the eldest son opened it, a picture of the Infante Don Juan, Prince of Asturias, in his naval uniform, was revealed, with a hand written message from the Prince: *For the family of the racer Francisco Cepeda, with all my affection, Juan.* There was also a longer, typed message from his secretary. Gerardo showed it to his father and Augustín called his family around him. Gerardo read the letter with a quivering voice.

> *Dear Sir*
>
> *His majesty, the Infante Don Juan, Prince of Asturias, has requested me to send you his most painful condolence, after the misfortune suffered by all of your family, owing to the loss of your brother, Francisco, in such an unfortunate accident. His majesty had the opportunity of meeting your brother in Paris, the day before the start of the competition that would cost him his life and, thus, he is among the last of the Spaniards who had the occasion to appreciate his gentlemanliness. We all regret this tragedy and you can rest assured that all Spaniards join the family in your pain. I beg you to forward to your brothers and sisters and the rest of the family that his majesty will not forget you in your enormous pain. I, personally, also join in this pain from all of my heart, as I was able to meet your brother the same day. I beg you to consider me as a true friend from now on.*
>
> *Yours sincerely,*
>
> *The Viscount of Rocamora, Secretary to Don Juan de Borbón*

Many years later, in 1941, when King Don Alfonso XIII died, Paco's father, Augustín, in a mutual show of respect, sent his condolences to the Prince, on behalf of the Cepeda family, never forgetting the Princes's kindness when his own son had died. Augustín received another letter of thanks from Don Juan de Borbón, who was still in exile, now in Rome, where his father had died, while Franco was ruling in Spain. Juan was now a father. His son, also called Juan, had been born in Rome in 1938 and would later return to his homeland as King Juan Carlos. The Prince wrote:

> *I deeply appreciate, along with all the royal family, your sincere condolence and loyal support that we have received after the death of His Majesty, the King Don Alfonso XIII, my unforgettable father (r.i.p.), role model for all Spaniards. They are a comfort for my pain and oblige my recognition.*
>
> *Rome, March 1941, Juan*

The Royal family had clearly not forgotten the Cepeda family. The mutual affection and affinity between the two families, one working class, from a small Basque town, the other Royal, which had been created by Paco's first meeting with the Prince, in Paris, before the start of the 1935 Tour, had remained over the years of pain and suffering.

21

THE QUESTION OF THE RIMS

I n the weeks following Paco's funeral, as the flowers on his grave began to wither and die, journalists continued to speculate on the causes of the accident and raised questions about the possible negligence of the organisers. There had been no official reaction to the accident from the organisers but there were rumours that Desgrange was considering removing some parts of the race the following year, and taking some action regarding the new equipment, considering the high number of mechanical failures. Paco's death had brought to attention what the French newspapers were calling, 'the rims incident', and the first stories began to circulate that Paco's deadly fall could have been caused by the use of duralumin in the wheels.

Paco's accident had immediately prompted the Aces to demand a return to the old wooden rims. Sylvère Maes, after finishing the stage to Grenoble, was reported to have said, 'If they don't change the duralumin rims, I will not start again. I don't want to die on the road. I have just almost had an accident. It's a miracle that I escaped crashing.'

On the twenty-ninth of July, when the Tour was finished

and Romain Maes had triumphed, an article by Pierre Marie, in *La Popularie*, the left-wing French newspaper, brought Paco's death back into sharp focus. He wrote:

'The 1935 Tour de France was a painful memory. From the beginning, it can be described with two words; 'hard-labour' and 'murderous'. Of the ninety-three that left Paris, less than fifty returned. There were many injuries, some of which were very serious, with one fatality. This, in short, is an assessment of the Tour.'

'It is always easy, of course to say this is Fate; take the intense heat during certain stages, the use of rims of an extra light metal that had not been adequately tested by the company, and the tyres that detached themselves from the rims because of inadequate adhesive, as was possibly the case in Cepeda's accident. In addition to these factors, there is the excessive fatigue brought about during the early stages, on the cobbles of the North, in the Vosges and in the Jura, where riders were pushing to establish a good ranking for themselves in the General Classification. Was it this that caused the mortal injury to Cepeda?'

'Whether these events caused or contributed to Cepeda's death is hypothesis but not entirely unlikely, when one considers that the physical demands on the body in the mountains have a disproportionate effect on the human body. When faced with unexpected situations, the rider is less able to react to the sudden change.'

Desgrange should have shouldered some of the blame. Each year, he had complained that the riders rode too slowly in certain stages. To others this seemed understandable given the severity of the race, but Desgrange had always demanded superhuman efforts from his riders and he expected nothing less than hard racing from start to finish. The reality was the riders were human and only had a certain amount of energy. They needed to measure their effort and recover a little, especially between two mountain stages or before or after a time trial. But the Tour had become big business and the welfare of the riders consequently suffered.

For Desgrange, the primary concern was the money and the profit he could generate from the sales of his newspaper. For most of the riders it was the same. They needed to make a living and earn as much money as they could from the Tour. Pélissier was a prime example. He chose to ride as an individual rather than for the French team, and when the French National team became depleted with abandonments, he declined promotion to the National team. He remained an individual because, as the Tour progressed, there were fewer and fewer individual riders to contest the prize money in that category, because more and more were being promoted to their National teams as the abandonments mounted up. Pélissier could make two or three thousand francs a day in prize money, according to the calculations of Monsieur Cazalis. The touristes-routiers were also calculating their earnings, while the Belgians were complaining they were winning less money than in previous years. Meanwhile, the business house advertising trucks were protesting because, after paying a million to *L'Auto* in cash, they were doing less business than they had done in previous years of the Tour. Money and commercialism dominated the Tour and it was a cruel irony that Paco Cepeda lost his life riding primarily for the pure pleasure of competing in what he believed was the greatest bike race in the world.

There were many journalists who argued that Cepeda's death could not simply be attributed to Fate. *Le Miroir des Sports,* a rival sports paper to Henri Desgrange's *L'Auto*, produced the following report with the headline, 'The Affair of the Rims'.

'After the Galibier stage, there were questions in the caravan about the metal rims. This year we know that the bikes were equipped with the duralumin rims, which are much lighter and more rigid than the commonly used wooden rims. But there was one thing that no-one had thought of, that during the descent from the cols, the repeated braking and the number, and the prolonged nature of them, caused the rims to heat up to such a point that the bands used to fix the tyres to the wheels would literally melt, so that the tyres rolled off the rims more easily than before.'

'The number of crashes involving Cepeda, Vignoli and Gestri were undoubtedly provoked by the abnormal detachment of the tyres, and that other riders did not fall victim to a brutal catastrophe was a miracle. Some riders, who had punctured, burned their fingers when changing their tubeless tyres because their wheels had heated up so much, and others, dreading a crash so much, did not hesitate to tie their tubeless tyres to the rims with extra binding, they were so worried about the tyres rolling off.'

It was rumoured that some of the top riders had already found wooden rims, the day after Cepeda's crash, and had used them for the next stage, from Grenoble to Gap, and for the remainder of the Tour. The other competitors, predominantly the touristes-routiers and the individuals, had to wait and continue to use the potentially deadly metal rims until enough wooden replacements could be sourced. The reality was that it was highly unlikely that enough wooden-rimmed wheels would be found before the finish in Paris. Riders had been struggling since the beginning of the Tour to find an adhesive which would keep the tubulars from rolling off the metal rims, particularly when the rims heated up with excessive braking, which they did on very hot days or on the long mountain descents. Danneels had found a remedy to fix the problem. He used shellac, as a glue, to stick his tyres to the rim. Paco, like most of the riders, was not aware of this and took his chances like everybody else.

There was criticism for the newspaper, *L'Auto*, which had bought, at good prices, what it thought to be the best equipment. However, there had been far too many problems, not only with the rims but also with the bottom brackets and the tubulars. The tyres were simply too thin for the often badly maintained roads. Monsieur Cazalis had reported ninety-six punctures on one stage.

Much of the criticism, which was heaped upon the organisation, came from the group of socialist and communist newspapers which had, for several years, tried to discredit the Tour de France, claiming that the riders were nothing but 'forçats' or manual workers who were being exploited by the capitalists of Desgrange, his newspaper *L'Auto* and the companies represented in the Caravan. Paco's death gave these papers the ammunition they needed to launch a new attack on the Tour. There was particular criticism at the lack of provision made by the organisers for individuals like Paco. If an individual rider had a mechanical failure, like a broken pedal or broken forks, there was no help for them, whereas the Aces would be given another bike. And the discrimination did not end there. Although the independents were given fifty francs a day in expenses, if they won a prime during a stage that was equal to, or more than their daily expenses, then they then had to forfeit their expenses.

Monsieur Desgrange was certainly an accomplished businessman, taking a thirty-three per cent cut of the race winnings. The company that supplied the duralumin rims had paid him five thousand francs for the privilege. And the medical company, which provided the ambulances and nurses, paid twenty-five thousand francs for the right to treat the riders on the road. Profit was Desgrange's main concern; the riders were an after thought.

The lack of clarity around what actually happened on the day of Paco's deadly fall was exacerbated by the poor media reporting, and the absence of an investigation by Desgrange. Four days after Paco's death, *Le Miroir des Sports*, published the details of that dramatic stage. A series of photographs appeared, claiming to show Paco being helped back onto his bike by spectators, following his accident. The pictures and captions suggested that, after 'crashing, Paco had staggered back to his feet and, with help from some spectators, had climbed back onto his bike and tried to continue, only to fall to the ground for a second time. The pictures also showed the Italian, Vignoli, standing in the background of the shot, his race over, after he had sustained a broken collar bone in the crash, which supposedly brought down Paco. On closer inspection, there is no doubt that Vignoli is standing in the background, but the rider in the foreground is not Paco Cepeda. It is, in fact, the race leader, Romain Maes.

The series of pictures actually show the aftermath of a collision between Vignoli and Maes. Paco's race number was sixty. Maes's number was six, but appeared as 06 on his back. Was this how the error was made? Whatever the reason, it was an appalling mistake by the newspaper and it typified the type of Tour reporting at the time. The spread of pictures made a great story but were part of a false account of what had actually happened. It is an example of the type of photo journalism which created many of the myths and legends that surround this iconic race. With riders spread out across the mountain, and the time gaps between the first and last riders sometimes more than an hour, it was impossible for reporters and photographers to witness all the action as it happened. Unless they were very lucky to be on the spot at the time of an accident, reporters had to piece together the action in the hotels, at the end of the stage, either by interviewing the riders or other officials or witnesses. These sources were not always reliable. Consequently, it was the myth that survived, whilst the truth lay buried and undisturbed in the years that followed.

It seemed unlikely that an independent investigation into Paco's crash and subsequent death would be held, and speculation and misinformation would be allowed to grow, until a spectator approached the Mayor of Livet and Gavet to report his concerns that a motor vehicle might have been the cause of Paco's fall.

22

REACTION AND INACTION

On the day after the accident, several witnesses commented on the conduct of a following car. It was reported to the Mayor of Livet and Gavet, on the evening of the eleventh of July, that a following car had been travelling too close to Cepeda as the riders had approached the bridge at Rioupéroux. The claim was made that the car had squeezed the space between Cepeda and the verge and had possibly made contact with him. This had caused him to crash and fall. The car had then continued on its way, failing to stop. When this was reported to him, the Mayor was obliged to inform the Public Prosecutor of Grenoble. He immediately opened a hearing and instructed local gendarmes to gather witness statements.

Had this report not been made, it is unlikely that there would have been any further investigations into Paco's accident. The likelihood is the fall would have been treated as something unfortunate but routine. It was something that had happened on a regular basis during the Tour that year but Desgrange had failed to take any action. Take Magne's accident for example. Too many vehicles were travelling amongst the riders and the ciné cameramen, who were a new addition to the Tour landscape, would take any risk to get the best shots. Their films, which were appearing in Paris cinemas, were already proving popular and were great publicity for the Tour, so it was unlikely that anything would change very quickly on that score.

Following the Mayor's referral to the Prosecutor, local police interviewed several witnesses to Paco's fall and a report into the accident was produced which can be viewed to this day. Paco's fall was seen by numerous spectators who had lined the roadside in the village of Rioupéroux, near to the incident. But, if ten people see the same accident, it is likely there will be ten different versions of the event.

Officers René Chevillard and Louis Faure arrived at the home of Monsieur Camille Quintin, aged sixty, the Mayor of Livet and Gavet, in Isere, in the early evening, following Paco's fall. The Mayor claimed to have heard, through rumours, that Paco had fallen on the outskirts of Rioupéroux, and he had been told that his front tyre had failed. The Mayor had not been in the vicinity of the accident so was not able to add anything to the officer's report. This visit was simply an official visit, in order to start the formal proceedings, to establish whether or not someone had purposely or inadvertently, through careless driving, caused Paco to fall.

The officers first witness was an engineer, Jean Maignet, aged thirty one, who lived in Rioupéroux. He had come out of the front of his house at about four in the afternoon, a little upstream from Rioupéroux's bridge, in order to watch the passing of the Tour de France. A compact group of riders, one of whom was Cepeda, came past. Several cars were following them. After the group disappeared, he saw a crowd of people running upstream. He followed them and arrived at the accident scene. At the scene, there were a great number of workers, including a number of foreign workers from the factory. A car, a cabriolet with the roof down, had stopped. By the time Maignet arrived at the site of the accident, drivers from the car had picked up Cepeda and were putting the cyclist into the back seat of the car. He knew that a doctor lived close by, but the drivers said that they preferred to take Cepeda to the closest hospital. He thought about taking the registration number of the car, which he scribbled down as 33HORD, but he could not be sure about that, as the car was already quite far away by the time he thought about taking down the number.

The next witness that the gendarmes interviewed was a fourteen year old baker's boy named Bernardinis, who was also from Rioupéroux. He said that he had taken up his position that afternoon on Route National at the southern end of Rioupéroux. He remembered seeing the accident clearly, as it happened fifty metres upstream from where he was standing. He was on the right hand side of the road and so had a clear view of the accident, as the cars were keeping to the left hand side of the road and so they did not obscure his view. There was a compact group of riders going at full speed in the direction of Grenoble, followed by a large number of cars. He thought that he saw the back tyre detach itself from the wheel of the last rider in the group, which caused Cepeda to fall to his left. At that instant, the car which was close behind him was unable to stop or avoid him and it struck him, sending him to the right hand side of the roadway. He then fell back onto the tramway which was set back from, and situated on the right hand side of the road. This car stopped immediately, as did the others behind it. There were three occupants in the car. They picked up the injured rider and placed him in their car and then started off straightaway in the direction of Grenoble, whilst the occupants of the second car picked up the bike of the stricken cyclist and placed it in their car. Both cars seemed to be official cars and the men seemed to be speaking amongst themselves in Spanish. He did not get the numbers of the cars.

His three friends, Tassile, Romano and Mattiussi were with him. Later, in a second statement to the police, he said that he could not be sure of all the details as there was so much going on, what with the cars, the people and all the dust kicked up by the accident.

Forty-nine year old, Antoine Vulpiano, a labourer, was positioned close to the incident on the outskirts of the village. He was on the left hand side of the road, about forty metres from the accident. He asserted that Cepeda fell because of the dangerous driving of a vehicle that was following the group which attempted to overtake them. Vulpiano claimed the vehicle struck and shunted Cepeda, making him fall violently onto the road surface. The vehicle was a red enclosed delivery van. Two following cars stopped immediately; one took Cepeda to hospital, whilst the other took his bike. When asked about the front wheel, he claimed that with all the confusion of the spectators, the cars, the riders and all the dust created, he could not see everything clearly. Vulpiano didn't inform the police about what he had seen immediately because he did not think that it was his duty, but he was convinced that the driver of the van was to blame.

Mattiussi, a thirty eight year old labourer, gave a statement that was identical to that of his friend, Vulpiano. He thought he was about thirty metres away from the accident and, from where he was, given that the road was very crowded and the cars were obscuring his view of the riders, he could not confirm that Cepeda was actually struck by a car. He just saw him fall by a car and that was all he knew.

An engineer, thirty one, Jean Maignet, could not add much to the investigation. He simply confirmed that the road was very crowded. The majority of people from Rioupéroux had positioned themselves on the right hand side of the road, to get a better view of the riders as they came through the village.

Ezekiel Blanco, was another witness who was interviewed.

He was a thirty-two-year-old, drinks delivery driver, living at 26 Rue de La Mutualitein, Grenoble. He had not seen the crash but he was informed about the accident by Antonio Prior when he arrived in Grenoble. He confirmed that Prior told him that Cepeda's fall was caused when he tried to accelerate away from the group at forty five kilometres per hour and that his tyre had rolled off and he had landed on his head in the fall. Blanco had known Cepeda quite well. He had helped to arrange a get together and celebrations for the Spanish team at the end of the stage when they had previously finished in Grenoble. Since Cepeda's death, he claimed he had been trying to help Cepeda's family deal with the consequences.

By far the clearest and most comprehensive statement came from a seventeen-year-old metal worker. Vanilio Tassile, who was watching the race, and was about five hundred metres downstream from the bridge at Rioupéroux when the accident happened, gave the following statement.

'When the group of about seven or eight riders had overtaken me and had travelled about forty metres, the last rider in the group gave a violent movement of the handlebars, swerved to the right and hit the road where he remained motionless and lifeless. Several following cars stopped straight away. I ran up and saw that the tyre on the front wheel of Cepeda's bike had detached itself from the rim and I am convinced that this must have been the cause of the accident. I am sure that no other car had overtaken the group or had caused the accident, so the tyre leaving the rim must have been the only reason for Cepeda to have fallen.'

He went on to confirm that the occupants of the first vehicle, a Torpedo, were Spanish, and that they took Cepeda to hospital. He was also certain that the two Italians, Vulpiano and Mattiussi, who were one hundred metres further upstream from him, could not have seen the accident clearly and he did not know anyone else at the scene, other than Bernardinis, who could say precisely what caused the fall. He repeatedly reaffirmed that the front tyre failure was the only cause of the accident and no car was involved. He did not warn the police because he did not want to interfere and because he thought that no one in particular was to blame.

Tassile later accompanied the gendarmes back to the scene of the crash. He took them to the bend in the road which was identified as the place where the horse chestnuts grow. However, by the time they visited the crash site, there was no evidence left of the accident. He helped with the construction of a detailed sketch of the accident. On the sketch, he identified exactly where he and Bernardinis had been standing and where Vulpiano and Mattiussi had been positioned. He showed the policeman the spot where Cepeda was when he lost control of the handle bars, which had kicked violently to the left. It was right in front of where he had been watching. He was quite definite that Cepeda had started out on the right hand side of the road and landed one metre from the ditch on the left hand side of the road. As the road was five metres in width, Cepeda had been catapulted four metres in a diagonal direction before hitting the ground. From where Vulpiano and Mattiussi had been standing, on the opposite side of the road, it was highly unlikely that they could have had a clear view of the accident. It was likely that the following cars would have obstructed their view. At a later interview, Tassile also claimed that it was impossible for him to be absolutely precise about the exact circumstances of the accident as the road was so full of cars and riders, and then spectators after the accident. It was only when he got closer to the bike, which lay in the road, that he saw the cause, which was the tyre peeling off the front wheel. He reaffirmed that no car attempted to pass the cyclists and the two cars that were closest to the riders were the cars occupied by the Spaniards who took Cepeda to hospital.

Antonio Prior visited Paco in the Bremer wing of the hospital the night of the accident. At that point, Paco had not had an operation. That was carried out the following day, just before midnight. Paco never fully regained consciousness and could never give a statement to the police. Prior claimed that Paco had not been in a coma when he had seen him and that he sounded as if he was trying to speak, but what he said was incomprehensible. By the time Paco's brother, Gerardo, arrived from Bilbao, Paco was not able to recognise him.

The two doctors who had treated Paco, Dr. Coutirier and Dr. Fermier, could not be interviewed by the police at the time they were compiling their evidence, as they were away from the hospital, and would not be returning to Grenoble until the end of September. When Doctor Fermier returned to Grenoble, he gave a statement, on the nineteenth of September, in which he reported that Cepeda was admitted with a fracture at the base of the skull which he considered was a consequence of a violent blow from a fall against the ground. Nothing would make him suspect or fear that Cepeda had been knocked off or struck by a vehicle. This immediately cast doubt on the testimonies of Vulpiano and Bernadinis, who had both claimed that they had seen him struck by a car or van.

The formal interview proceedings ended on the ninth of November with the final statement delivered by Paco's Spanish teammate, Antonio Martinez Prior.

'On the eleventh of July, 1935, a little before arriving in Grenoble, and when I was in a group made up of several riders, notably Cepeda, who was leading the said group, I noticed him making a break in order to catch the end of the peloton. A little after having overtaken him, I heard the noise of a fall and turning round I saw my compatriot, Cepeda, was lying on the floor. I cannot say exactly how he fell, nor for what reason, because we carried on with the intention of getting to the finishing line. So I don't know if he was struck by a car, and in any event, I didn't see anything.'

By the thirty first of January 1936, the investigations into the accident had been completed and a decision had been made as to whether any culpable manslaughter charges could be brought.

The magistrate's official report stated that, 'no information has been uncovered to give sufficient grounds for official manslaughter charges to be brought against anyone who, at Rioupéroux, on the eleventh of July 1935, either by negligence, careless or dangerous driving, or by breaking any rules of the highway code, caused the death of the cyclist Cepeda. It has also been established that it is impossible to determine, in an exact way, the causes of Cepeda's fall.'

Officially, this final statement drew the tragic story of Francisco Cepeda to a close. Whilst it initially seemed to be a favourable outcome for Henri Desgrange and the Tour organisation, it did nothing to end speculation around the causes of Paco's accident and subsequent death.

In another completely separate incident, a criminal court reached its verdict on an accident which occurred at Jarrie, in Isere, during the Tour. The crowd had overrun the road, leaving a tightly packed, narrow channel for the riders and the following vehicles to pass through. A motorcyclist, Louis Grangeat, lost control of his bike and was thrown into the spectators, injuring six of them. The court considered that the responsibility should be shared between the motorcyclist and the public, the public having acted imprudently by swarming onto the road. This separate incident, along with the crashes of Vignoli and later Camusso, who was severely injured when he was hit by a truck on the stage to Nice, served to illustrate how dangerous the Tour had become for riders, spectators and support vehicles. It was growing in complexity and Desgrange had less control over his race than ever before.

Jean Roussel, who had immersed himself in the history of the Tour de France since he was a child and is the author of *Il était une fois Le Tour de France*, made the point that, 'if Cepeda's death is reported at all by the historians in the numerous books about the Tour de France, it is only mentioned in a most superficial manner.' Most references to it are also inaccurate, particularly regarding the place and manner of the accident. In many of the history books about the Tour, it is generally reported that Francisco Cepeda plunged spectacularly into a ravine, whilst descending the Galibier. Whilst this version of the story may add to the drama and mythology of the Tour, it strays from the truth. Roussel concludes that, so often, in the reporting of the Tour, 'epic unreality triumphs over reality, and silence has the upper-hand over truth.'

However, it is not only the historians or the journalists of the day who were guilty of embellishing or misinterpreting the truth. It was often in the interests of the Tour organisation itself to be economical with the truth, not only to promote and create a mythology around the race but also to safeguard the integrity of the Tour, or, more dramatically, to protect its very future and existence against the growing voices of opposition.

Raymond Huttier, of *Le Miroir des Sports*, was a particular critic of the dubious goings on between the constructors and the riders from 1929. Desgrange was not only often disgruntled with the manufacturers but also the riders, who he thought were trying to wrestle power away from him. This is what led to him setting up national teams in 1930. For nearly a decade Huttier was one of the Tour's fiercest critics, denouncing the conditions imposed upon the riders and the brutality of some of the routes. Of Paco, he wrote:

'Cepeda was no star of the Tour de France. Riding as an Individual, one of about twenty, invited by Desgrange, he was in the Spanish B team. In the event that the Spanish A team lost any of its riders during the race, there was the possibility, within the rules devised by Desgrange, that Cepeda could be promoted to the A team. He was under contract to Desgrange and was provided with a bike, the yellow bike provided by *L'Auto* to all the riders, as well as some equipment; twenty tyres and some daily expenses of one hundred francs. This was nothing compared to the package offered to the elite riders, known as the Aces. Riders like Cepeda were nevertheless integral to the race, as they bulked out the field, and were also good enough riders to provide some stiff competition for the classier riders who were eventually going to contest the podium positions. Cepeda's outstanding performance on the Galibier, in 1930 was evidence of his ability on any given day to spring a surprise but he was never going to threaten the overall standings and would do well to make it to the Parc des Princes. As such, Desgrange paid Cepeda, and individual and touristes-routiers riders like him, little attention.'

Huttier described Cepeda as, 'a gentle, young man, a kind and pleasant boy, with eyes like hot coals and a beaming smile.'

What Huttier admired about Paco was that he raced in the Tour for the sheer joy of it and his passion for riding came above everything else. His father was proud of his achievements but, like any parent, was probably anxious about his son's safety, in what was a potentially dangerous sport.

After Cepeda's death there was wide criticism of the organisers of the Tour, accusing them of only being interested in what the big names were doing, while those who were victims of misfortune had to face their difficulties on their own.

The person who should have been most interested in discovering the truth was the director of the race himself. If Desgrange had held a thorough investigation of his own, separate from the police investigation, he may have been able to quieten the accusations levelled at him by those who believed that the riders, especially those not part of the French team, had been abandoned by the organisation. However, because Desgrange largely ignored the causes of the accident, speculation about the role of the duralumin rims would not go away and reporters continued to direct their criticism towards him and his organisation.

On the twenty-sixth of July 1935, a report appeared in *L'Aero* entitled 'Fall after Fall on the Tour' which laid out the major concerns. It began,

'Cepeda dead, Antonin Magne, Danneels, Neuville, Camusso, Merviel, a dozen others seriously injured and the Tour de France has lost some of its very best riders. The crashes have depleted it. And, since those losses, nothing has changed; uncertainty has remained. Since Marseille, the 'dramas', 'the beautiful staging', 'the newspaper' have all taken a big hit.'

The report went on to explore the possible reasons for the falls. The number of punctures could not be dismissed and then there was the issue of the rims. The tubes were leaving the rims too often and that resulted in spectacular falls. The lightness of the duralumin rims needed to be looked at, as well as the insulating tape that stuck the tyre to the rim. Since the beginning of the Tour there was evidence that excessive heat liquified the coated fabric which stuck the tube to the rim. This happened because it had tar at its base. Consequently, the tube did not stick and when the rider made a sudden turn the tube slid. The rider then lost control of his bike because he was riding on the metal rim.

The problems related to the heat and the rider's thirst were also raised. Some of the riders were forced to repeatedly take on different fluids, including beers or spirits, which would have led to a lack of control or lowered their sense of danger and good judgement. The report also did not rule out that the wholehearted commitment of the riders might have resulted in what was referred to as, 'additional excitement' or 'a little too much action.' This Tour had been the fastest in history. The dangers intensified and more mistakes and miscalculations happened when speeds increased.

The report finished by highlighting the role played by the Tour convoy in the accidents. It singled out and accused the mounted photographers and the ciné cameramen, who were competing with each other for the best shots. In doing so, their behaviour was, at times, 'audacious' and 'too bold, nurturing danger.' There were also too many vehicles. The report concluded, 'Since Mr Desgrange must have his rules, he should draw up a chapter on discipline. The publicity for his Tour de France would not be seriously affected but there would be fewer challenges to his interests.'

Today, as riders pass the place where Paco fell, and they often do, both professionals and enthusiastic amateurs, heading to, or from, the epic climb of Alp d'Huez, they would not know the significance of this bend in the road, identified, at the time, as the place where the horse chestnuts grow. And who can blame them? For, no monument or memorial was erected there to record how, one late summer afternoon, in early July, eighty-eight years ago, a likeable young Spaniard, with a good-natured smile, lost his life, in pursuit of a dream he could not surrender. The horse chestnuts still mark the spot but what they saw on that fateful day, will never be truly known.

AFTERWORD: IN SEARCH OF PACO

I began my journey to establish the true facts surrounding the death of Francisco Cepeda in 2014, but Paco's story might never have been told. In 2020, while out on a bike ride, I suffered a life changing event which drew me even closer to Paco's tragic narrative.

It's November 2020, it's minus two degrees and I'm lying on a grass verge, on a single-track lane, still clipped into my pedals. I'm unconscious. I'm not breathing, There is no pulse. I'm gone.

I remember nothing of that day. In fact, the previous two days, before my cardiac arrest, have also been completely wiped from my memory. The only person who has a clear memory of that terrible day is the person who saved my life, my wife, Jo.

That morning we had woken to brilliant sunshine and a bluebird sky. In spite of the cold, we decided to go for a ride. We didn't often ride together, especially in the winter. Jo preferred to run, so most of my riding was done alone. In fact, two days earlier, I had done a seventy kilometre ride around the country lanes of Somerset and Wiltshire. On this occasion, because of the temperature, we had decided to do a short, off-road ride. Jo would take her electric mountain bike and I took my cyclo-cross bike.

We headed off, down the hill, towards the Kennet and Avon canal, where we intended to pick up the tow path and head towards Bradford-on-Avon. As we started our descent, the view opened up and the scene was spectacular. We were in bright sunlight, but the river valley below was shrouded in thick mist. We stopped to take a picture because it looked so mystical.

Once we plunged into the mist, the temperature dropped significantly. Our faces, fingers and toes complained bitterly. After riding a couple of kilometres along the tow path, the off-road ride no longer seemed such a good idea, so we decided on a change of plan. We would leave the tow path and head back up the hill, into the sunlight and the winter warmth.

We left the canal, joined the main road and began to climb. The effort alone was sure to warm us up. The climb to the top was just over a kilometre. It averages nine point two per cent but has some steep ramps of almost seventeen per cent. This wasn't a problem for Jo on her electric bike but was a challenge for me, as the gearing on the cyclo-cross bike wasn't really suited to a road climb like this. Nevertheless I struggled and strained my way to the top, where we turned off the road into a narrow lane. Blackberry Lane led to a network of lanes which we knew would all be bathed in crisp, morning sunshine.

A couple of hundred metres along the lane we stopped outside the gates of a racing stables. Still astride our bikes, we leaned against the stone wall to take in the view. A grey BMW came through the gates and the driver smiled and waved at us. Turning back to look at the view, Jo suddenly sensed an uneasy silence and, turning back to me, saw me slumped against the wall. Instinct immediately told her that something was seriously wrong. She quickly eased me to the ground and unclipped me from my pedals. She knew I had suffered a cardiac arrest. She didn't need to check my breathing, or look for a pulse, as she knew there would be none. Knowing she had left her mobile phone at home, she quickly pulled mine from the back pocket of my jacket. She entered the code, phoned 999, explained the situation, gave our location to the operator and then informed him she was going to put the phone down in order to start CPR.

As each second passed, my life was slipping away but it was my good fortune that Jo was with me that morning. As a personal trainer, she had been trained in CPR multiple times. It was also my good fortune that, in that moment of crisis and terror, she was able to hold her nerve and put every atom of her being into saving my life. She started pressing forcefully on my chest in steady rhythms.

Realising she was completely alone, Jo, repeatedly, shouted for help, as loud as she could but, knowing this was an isolated spot and there may be no help, she quickly returned to the compressions, applying firm pressure to my chest.

'Come on Mike! Come on Mike! You can do this! You can do this! Come on Mike! Come on Mike!'

Jo chanted this mantra as she worked. Somewhere deep inside, she thought I would hear her and that, after years and years of racing and training together, she knew these words would mean something to me. She knew that if I could hear these words, I would respond and do everything I could to stay with her.

She continued like this for three or four minutes before two young women came running from the stables. One, by chance, happened to be a physiotherapist. She was able to take over the CPR, as the operator had sensed that Jo's efforts were slowing. The second woman ran back down the lane, to the main road, to guide the ambulance into the lane when it arrived.

About twelve minutes passed before the wailing siren was

heard. My two guardian angles continued to work in tandem until the paramedics were at my side. At this point, Jo had to stand back. She could do no more. I was quickly hooked up to a defibrillator and shocked. It worked and, for the first time in almost a quarter of an hour, there was a pulse. Soon a doctor from the Wiltshire Air Ambulance arrived on the scene. She advised that I should be ventilated and stabilised at the road side, before being moved to the hospital in Bath.

Watching the doctor at work, Jo, who had been chanting her words throughout, suddenly stopped. The enormity of what was happening was beginning to sink in. She was now a spectator and felt powerless to help me. My life was now in the hands of others. Shock was beginning to take hold when the doctor suddenly brought her back to the present.

'Keep going.' she said. 'Keep talking to him. He may be able to hear you.'

Once stabilised, I was rushed to the hospital in Bath. A policewoman had also arrived at the scene. She took Jo and they went ahead of the ambulance, sirens blaring through the mist. Once in Accident and Emergency, I was quickly assessed and then rushed through for an MRI to ascertain the damage to my heart. From there it was straight to the theatre for surgery. One of my arteries was completely blocked and required stenting. Three of the doctors who were treating me were keen cyclists and seeing a seemingly fit and lithe cyclist lying in front of them, now clinging to life, must have shocked them to the core. For months, I had been in full training for a spring triathlon and, prior to this event, I had been reaching my peak fitness. Now the odds were stacked against me surviving the end of the day.

I had been ventilated at the roadside because of the length of time that I had been without oxygen and, after surgery, I would need to be moved to Critical Care and heavily sedated for further observation. Miraculously, I survived the night and the following day, but my troubles were only just beginning.

Within days, my health had taken a serious turn for the worse. First, I developed aspirational pneumonia and then sepsis. We were in the middle of Covid and a lockdown had been imposed so no visitors were allowed. My situation was becoming increasingly hopeless. The infection had taken hold of my body and the doctors, fearing I would not survive another night, allowed my wife to visit. She stayed at my bedside until daybreak, talking to me, playing my favourite music, willing and praying for me to pull through. By morning, I was stable again and my wife was able to go home. Another miracle.

As Christmas Day approached, my condition continued to hang in the balance. My kidneys had failed and I had developed multiple blood clots on my lungs. Attempts to reduced my sedation, to assess my cognitive responses, ended in failure, as I quickly became distressed. Running out of options, the doctors decided to take me back into surgery to see if they had missed something. Considering my condition, this was a very risky procedure and prompted another compassionate visit from my wife and two sons. I was still heavily sedated and remember nothing of the visit but it must have been heart wrenching for my family to see me lying there, shrouded in tubes and wires. Would they ever see me again?

I survived the procedure and the doctors were satisfied that they had missed nothing. It would now be a waiting game to see whether I could fight off the pockets of infection. To allow the doctors to assess my cognitive abilities, the ventilator was removed and I was given a tracheotomy, to help me breathe and allow the sedation to be steadily lifted. My kidneys were still badly compromised but, gradually, my condition began to improve and the infection subsided.

By early in the new year, I was finally out of danger. I was sitting up for the first time and sipping water from a teaspoon. By the second week in January, I was moved to the cardiac ward where, within a few days, I caught Covid. This came as a crushing blow after everything I had been through, but providence decreed that my symptoms would be mild. My kidneys were slowly beginning to recover and the likelihood of needing dialysis waned. It seemed that I was finally out of the woods but I had one more procedure, before my discharge on the second of February; the fitting of an implantable cardioverter defibrillator (ICD)

I spent sixty-nine days in hospital, forty-two of those in Critical Care. I owe my life, initially to Jo and the young women from the racing stables, and then the paramedics and the doctor at the scene, but there is no doubt that I would not have survived this terrible experience without the skill, dedication and expertise of the doctors and nurses in Critical Care. Of the many specialists who treated me, only one thought I had any chance of survival. Lying in a coma for more than three weeks, the odds were stacked heavily against me, as they had been against Paco. I've often thought that, if Paco had been able to receive the same level of critical care that I received, he might also have survived. As I recovered from my ordeal and eventually found myself riding my bike again, my desire to tell Paco's untold story, felt stronger than ever.

But what stimulated my interest in Francisco Cepeda's story in the first place? As a teenage boy, my imagination had been sparked by the grainy black and white images of riders toiling up Alpine climbs on ITV's *World of Sports*, half hour, Tour de France highlights show, on a Saturday lunchtime. Eddy Merckx and Bernard Thévenet battling it out on the slopes of the Galibier or the Col d'Izord. These epic encounters led me towards my local cycling club, where my training began in earnest in the hope of following in the footsteps of my heroes. There was something pure about this sport. I had already competed in many different sports teams, but cycling seemed to have a simplicity which appealed to me — the rider, the bike, the road and whatever the elements could throw at you. Then there was the freedom you experienced each time you set out on a ride.

I think similar feelings attracted Paco to cycling and led to his dream of riding the Tour de France. He achieved his dream, whereas I only raced the Tour on my training rides. Often training alone, I would pass the time by imagining myself in a lone breakaway or being dropped by the peloton, only to claw my way back, and then attack again on a climb, leaving my rivals in my wake.

My dreams of a career in cycling ended in my second year at university. The closest I came to riding at the top level came on my training rides across the Yorkshire Wolds with my training partner, Mark Robinson, a top amateur in the late seventies and early eighties, who had ridden for Great Britain in the famous Peace Race, an amateur race, behind the Iron Curtain, which rivalled the Tour de France in terms of its difficulty and the crowds it drew. Mark and I would meet on crisp autumn and winter mornings and ride out from Hull through Beverley, then across the Wolds to Market Weighton, Malton or Pocklington, near York, and then trace the Humber back to Hull.

Even though he gave me a proper hiding on those rides, I came out of the winter pretty strong and with high hopes of making a breakthrough in the spring and summer road races around Yorkshire. In my first criterium in Hartlepool, I was literally brought down to earth. When riding in the middle of the peloton, another rider cut across in front of me and took my front wheel away. I flew through the air spectacularly, landing on my hands and then rolling over onto to my side. My first race of the season was over. I spent the afternoon in the General Hospital, before an uncomfortable car journey back to

Hull that evening. I was lucky nothing was broken and I didn't land on my head. The foam racing hats we wore in road races in the seventies didn't offer much protection.

Undaunted, I returned to riding two weeks later and by my own standards had quite a good summer, riding my first stage race, finishing fifth in the County Championships and riding some good races at the Isle of Man international cycling week. But reality slowly dawned and I realised that I wasn't going to be able to study for an English degree and cycle four hundred miles a week. My flirtation with road racing ended and I decided that I needed to concentrate on my studies.

I never lost my love of riding, putting my experience to good use in my twenties by turning to triathlon, a new sport, in its infancy in the United Kingdom. I was riding every day, either commuting to my job as a teacher or riding simply for the sake of it. Whether it be riding up a mountain or along a country lane, riding a bike has always given me that feeling of what it means to be truly alive. I like to imagine that Paco had similar feelings.

Years later, married with three boys, my wife and I fulfilled a dream that we had been nurturing for many years by buying a small apartment in the French Alps. We chose the ski resort of Valloire. We both loved to ski but when we were looking for a place to buy, my wife was unaware that Valloire was also in the heart of Tour de France country, sandwiched between the Col du Télégraphe and the Col du Galibier and close to many other major Alpine climbs. In the winter, we could ski, and, in the summer, Valloire would be the perfect base from which to ride hundreds of kilometres of mountain roads and cols. Valloire is also an excellent base from which to follow the Tour de France, as the Galibier has been crossed sixty-three times since it was first used in the 1911 Tour. It is the fifth most visited climb in Tour history.

Many titanic cycling battles have taken place on the Galibier. In recent times, Marco Pantani's audacious attack, in torrential rain, to take the race lead from the German, Jan Ullrich, is one of the most famous and celebrated. Valloire is close to the Italian border and there is something of a love affair with the Pirate, as Pantani was known. So much so, there is a monument to him about half way up the climb. It is there because it was at this point, five point five kilometres from the summit of the Galibier, that Marco Pantani launched his attack. 1998 was the year, and the Tour had already been rocked by the Festina Affair. When a Belgian soigneur, working for the Festina team, was stopped on the border between Belgium and France, four hundred doping products were found in his car. The Festina team and management were not immediately implicated and, with the team protesting their innocence, the Tour director, Jean-Marie Leblanc, allowed them to continue in the race. However, when the Festina team director and doctor, Eric Ryckaert, were also arrested and questioned by police, it became clear that the Festina team was being doped under the supervision of the team management. At this point, on the eve of stage seven, the individual time trial, Leblanc did finally do the right thing and throw the Festina team out of the Tour.

For better or for worse, the Tour continued and brought us to stage fifteen, from Grenoble to Les Deux Alpes, and Pantani's extraordinary ride. Pantani started the day with a three minute, eleven second deficit on the race leader Jan Ullrich. After his attack, he had almost wiped out that deficit when he reached the top of the Galibier. By the time he had made the long descent to the bottom of Les Deux Alpes, Pantani had a four minute lead. On the final climb of nine kilometres, in his trademark bandana and his yellow sunglasses perched on his head, Pantani gained a further thirty seconds per kilometre on Ulrich, to finish the stage nearly nine minutes clear of his rival. Bobby Julich, who finished third in the Tour that year, said, 'I knew Pantani was dangerous but I didn't think that he could do what he did today. He made us all look silly.'

Some of the fastest stages in Tour history were ridden that year, but all of that is forgotten. What is remembered is that the charismatic Italian, Marco Pantani, achieved the impossible, producing a ride with time gaps that were not thought possible in the modern era of the Tour. Despite the fact Pantani was later banned for doping and died, alone, in a hotel room from a drugs overdose, his memory is honoured with a monument on the Galibier. That puzzles me. So often we remember what we care to remember and forget what we care to forget.

When I first became interested in Francisco Cepeda's death, I was curious to find the whereabouts of the memorial to him. Most of the history books on The Tour de France, if they report his death at all, claim that he plunged into a ravine while descending the Galibier. There are so many memorials to Tour de France riders, I naturally assumed there would be one to the first rider to die in the Tour, and it would probably be at the site where he had fallen.

I thought I knew the Galibier fairly well, having ridden up and down it from both sides on many occasions. There is of course the huge monument to Henri Desgrange, on the Lautaret side of the Galibier, just below the tunnel, built in 1949, but I had never seen another memorial on the mountain.

In the summer of 2014, making several trips from our home in Valloire, I made a painstaking survey of the mountain road, from the summit of the Galibier to Vizelle near Grenoble, knowing that Paco's accident must have taken place somewhere between the two. Using what few leads I had from newspaper reports, my journey eventually brought me to the small and sleepy village of Rioupéroux. Here, I visited the local museum, in the village centre, but they had no knowledge of the accident.

It was a baking hot day and the back streets of the village were deserted and dusty, much like they must have been on the day that Paco fell. I was looking for the old road which I thought the race must have used and I was also looking for a point in the road, near a drop off, or ravine, where the accident might have happened. I had no luck. There wasn't any sign of life and most of the houses had their windows shuttered. I was about to leave, when a wizened old lady peered between the rusty stays of a pair of elegant, iron gates. She wanted to know what I was looking for.

'Have you lived here long?' I asked in my basic French.

'All my life,' she replied.

My hopes were immediately raised. She must have been in her late eighties, so she would have been alive at the time of the accident. Even though she would have been a little girl or even a baby, a father or an uncle might have talked about that terrible accident in July 1935.

'You know the Tour de France?'

'Of course,' she replied.

'I'm trying to find the place where an accident happened, in the Tour de France, in 1935. It happened somewhere near here. The first rider to die in the Tour de France. Do you know anything?'

She thought for a moment and looked at me as if she was about to reveal something she had heard long ago. But then she shook her head.

'No. I am sorry. I never heard anything about an accident. I like the Tour de France. I follow the Tour de France. Where are you from?'

'I'm from England.'

'Oh! Chris Froome. I like Chris Froome. I hope he wins the

Tour this year.' She raised her hand and waved. 'Well, enjoy your ride.'

Her ancient voice trailed off as she made her way back down her garden path.

I returned to England later that summer, having made no progress in my search for either a memorial to Paco or the site of the accident.

Little did I know then, but the museum I had visited was less than eight hundred metres from the place where Paco fell. It would be almost three years before I would make this discovery.

Before that, in June 2015, my quest to find out more about Paco led me to his birthplace in Sopuerta, in Biscay, Northern Spain. My wife and I stayed in a bed and breakfast, over-looking the small settlement, half way up the hill which Paco trained on and must have ridden a thousand times. On our first morning, we awoke to find a fine mist hanging over the valley. A herd of goats were on the road, outside the house, feeding on the fresh summer grass on the verges. Other than the occa-sional tinkle from their bells, life seemed undisturbed. I could picture Paco riding up this hill, at the start of one of his morning training rides. After breakfast, we made our way to the cemetery, where we found Paco's grave in the far corner. Next to him lay his brother Primitivo, who had tragically died shortly after him, from tuberculosis. How the Cepeda family must have suffered at that time. As I entered the gates, I had a feeling that his story and my journey were just beginning.

It was an impressive grave, with a carving of Paco's smiling face on the headstone. I felt that this moment was an important milestone in my journey, to tell his untold story. From there, we went to the church of San Pedro, where we lit a candle in his memory and spent some time in quiet contemplation. The village was quiet but its impressive tourist information centre was open so we went inside and explained why we had come to

Sopuerta. Panchi, who worked there, spoke excellent English. There was very little about Paco in the museum but she explained that her father, Javier, who had been mayor of Sopuerta, had written an article about Paco and he might be able to meet with me the following day. She would ask him.

Encouraged by this new lead, we spent the afternoon exploring the surroundings. The Cepeda family home has long since gone but in its place is a tree, beneath which there is a monument to Paco. Appropriately sculpted from iron, the memorial represents Paco holding a broken wheel, reinforcing the belief, in Spain at least, that the accident was caused by a faulty rim. The afternoon was spent exploring the derelict kilns on the edge of Sopuerta, their red brick chimneys now crumbling and overgrown with brambles and bushes. This was once a thriving community with a population of three and a half thousand, much greater than it is today.

I spent an hour and a half with Javier the following morning listening to his stories. He had known Paco's sister, Espe, the youngest of the Cepeda children. He had also done some research into the accident and had written an article for a local Basque magazine. I left with some photocopies of articles and pictures, as well as Javier's article. My journey to Bilbao and Biscay had brought me closer to Paco and inspired me to get his untold story written.

On returning home, I devoured every book I could find on the Tour de France in order to learn more about the 1935 Tour and Paco's fatal accident. I discovered a great deal about the history of the Tour and the lives of some of the Tour's greatest riders and the dramatic twists and turns of this iconic race, but little or nothing about Francisco Cepeda. I soon found myself at a dead end. I did not have enough information for an article let alone a book. Time moved on and the project began to run out of steam.

It was now February 2017 and I was on the point of giving

up. At a loose end, one winter evening, in one final attempt to kick start my project, I went back to the internet. Searching for any film footage of the 1935 Tour de France, I came across one short film sequence taken of the early stages of the 1935 Tour. It contained no shots of Paco and was of limited use to me, but something caught my eye. On the message board, beneath the video, was a single comment which read, 'I am the great nephew of Francisco Cepeda and would like to know if anyone has found any more film footage of the 1935 Tour.' Alvaro Rey Cepeda. Were my fortunes about to change?

This seemed too good to be true. I immediately emailed Alvaro, explaining my interest in his great uncle and my desire to write his story and see a monument erected to him, in France, at or near the site of the accident. To my relief, Alvaro replied very quickly and once the connection had been made, I immediately sensed that a book about Paco was a real possibility. Alvaro was curious to know why I was interested in his great uncle. I replied:

'You may ask why I am interested in the story. I am now fifty-eight, but I have been cycling and racing since I was fifteen. Like Francisco, I was a good amateur. Not as good as him, and not good enough to be a professional, but I was very serious. I loved riding for its own sake and dreamed of riding as a professional. Instead, I became an English teacher, but I continued to ride my bike and read stories about cycling. Ten years ago, I bought a small apartment near Valloire, on the Col du Galibier and I became interested in his story. I was amazed that in the history books on the Tour de France there is often no mention of Francisco, or perhaps only one or two sentences, and, even then, the information is inaccurate. So, I started my investigation and then I learned about the wheel rims, and the multiple crashes that day and then the silence after the accident. I can perhaps understand the silence in 1935, because his death would not be good publicity for Henri

Desgrange and the Tour, but I do not understand the silence in recent years. If Francisco was French then there would be a monument but, even now, the Tour de France does not want any bad publicity, and I think that it would be difficult for the organisation to recognise him today. The question would be asked, 'Why has it taken so long? and there is no good answer to this question. But this is not a good reason to give up.

I feel I have something in common with Francisco - his passion, his sense of fairness, his determination to succeed (particularly in the 1935 Tour when so many Spanish riders had already abandoned) and this is why I want to write his story and the truth about the 1935 Tour.'

Alvaro explained that he was the grandson of Fernando, Paco's brother. Alvaro's grandmother and grandfather had lived opposite the Cepeda's house and his mother, Adeline, was their only daughter. Alvaro had collected photographs of Paco and had many newspaper reports from French and Spanish newspapers and magazines covering Paco's career. Most importantly, he had discovered that the original police investigation report into the accident still existed in the Isère Archives Department. Ironically, at the same time that I was visiting Sopuerta in 2015, in search of Paco's grave and birthplace, Alvaro was in Grenoble, with a friend, Josu, who lived in Toulouse, in search of the police report, in the hope that it might enable him to identify the exact spot where his great uncle had fallen. He too, along with his uncles, had dreamed of placing a memorial to Paco in France. They were not allowed a copy of the file but they were allowed to photograph it. Significantly, the file contained a sketch of the accident site, on the outskirts of Rioupéroux. It identified the bend as 'the virage des châtaigniers', the bend with the chestnuts. Those words, and a little help from two local women, enabled Alvaro and Josu to find the bend where Paco fell. It must have been very emotional moment for Alvaro.

We continued to share information over the following months and, it goes without saying that, without Alvaro's help, this book would not have been written. In July 2018, I was able to visit the site of the accident myself. Now the road is a busy national route linking Grenoble to Briançon, and France with Italy. In summer, the area attracts cyclists, paragliders and hikers and, in winter, skiers. The traffic thunders past this fateful spot and, judging from the little grotto, adorned with flowers and pictures of a loved one on the opposite side of the road, another family has grieved the loss of a someone dear to them.

Although, this bend was the place where Paco's life was cruelly taken from him, this was no place for a memorial. I had promised Alvaro that, in addition to writing Paco's story, I would do whatever I could to help the family erect a memorial to him. With that in mind, I had already met with the Mayor of Livet and Gavet, that summer, to establish whether, in principle, such an idea would be supported by the local community. He was enthusiastic about the idea and the following summer, we agreed on a site for a memorial, in the centre of Riouperoux, near to the museum. That project is still in progress, as I write, but I am hopeful that a fitting memorial might be completed in the near future.

Paco was the first of only three riders to die during the race. Tommy Simpson, who was the first British rider to wear the yellow jersey, became the second fatality when he collapsed and died during his ascent of Mont Ventoux, on the thirteenth stage of the 1967 Tour de France. Like Paco, he was only twenty-nine years old. There is a memorial on the Ventoux near to where he fell and this has since become a place of pilgrimage for thousands of cyclists. The memorial is made of granite and bears the silhouette of a racing cyclist. It was the idea of *Cycling Weekly's* editor, Alan Gayfer, who made an appeal to his magazine's readers which raised one thousand five hundred pounds. It was unveiled in 1969, two years after Simpson died. The last rider to die in the Tour de France was the Italian rider Fabio Casartelli. He was only twenty-four years old. As an amateur, he became Olympic champion in 1992 and turned professional in 1993. Two years later, riding with Lance Armstrong in the Motorola team, he crashed on the descent from the Col de Portet d'Aspet, during stage fifteen. Casartelli's head struck a roadside concrete block and he sustained fatal injuries. The Société du Tour de France and the Motorola team placed a memorial close to where he crashed. The memorial is a sundial, arranged so the shadow of the sun highlights three dates — his birth, his death and the day he won his Olympic gold medal. Francisco Cepeda Nistal has a memorial where his home once stood in Sopuerta and this book is my tribute to him, but my hope is that, after eighty-eight years, his memory will, one day, also be rightfully acknowledged, both in France and by the Tour de France.

A young star in the making

Paco crashes while leading the fifth G.P of Biscay before finishing third

Paco follows Ricardo Montereo with José Garcia on his wheel

Paco, second in line, track racing

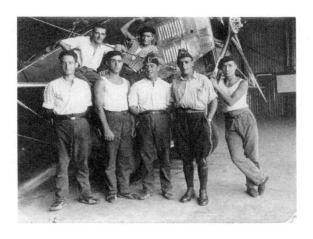

Paco, second from right, on military service in Morocco

Paco's funeral procession. Vicente Trueba holds a ribbon in the foreground

ABOUT THE AUTHOR

Michael Thompson is a retired English teacher and a former amateur cyclist, triathlete and runner. *The Final Descent is* his first book and the process of researching and writing it has taken almost nine years. He lives in Bath and is married to Jo, a former international athlete. They have three sons and one grandson.

Michael Thompson can be contacted through Twitter, Instagram and TikTok or by emailing: bikingtommo@gmail.com

twitter.com/BikingTommo

instagram.com/bikingtommo

tiktok.com/@bikingtommo

Printed in Great Britain
by Amazon

41250923R00158